In Five Eyes

Selected previous publications by Andrew Duncan

Poetry

In a German Hotel
Cut Memories and False Commands
Sound Surface
Alien Skies
*Switching and Main Exchange**
*Pauper Estate**
Anxiety before Entering a Room. New and selected poems
Surveillance and Compliance
Skeleton Looking at Chinese Pictures
The Imaginary in Geometry
*Savage Survivals (amid modern suavity)**
*Threads of Iron**

Criticism

The Poetry Scene in the Nineties (internet only)
Centre and Periphery in Modern British Poetry
The Failure of Conservatism in Modern British Poetry
Origins of the Underground
*The Council of Heresy**
*The Long 1950s**
Fulfilling the Silent Rules (forthcoming)

As editor

Don't Stop Me Talking (with Tim Allen)
Angel Exhaust (magazine: 1992–98 and 2005–   )
Joseph Macleod: *Cyclic Serial Zeniths from the Flux*

*Shearsman titles

In Five Eyes

Andrew Duncan

Shearsman Books

First published in the United Kingdom in 2013 by
Shearsman Books
50 Westons Hill Drive
Emersons Green
Bristol
BS16 7DF

Shearsman Books Ltd Registered Office
30–31 St. James Place, Mangotsfield, Bristol BS16 9JB
(this address not for correspondence)

http://www.shearsman.com/

ISBN 978-1-84861-272-3

Copyright © Andrew Duncan, 1992, 2003, 2013.

The right of Andrew Duncan to be identified as the author
of this work has been asserted by him in accordance with the
Copyrights, Designs and Patents Act of 1988.
All rights reserved.

Contents

Author's Note 7

Sound Surface

Suspended Section 11
Hanging Around 12
Meet a New God 13
Circular 14
Clipping and Shear 17
Consciousness From Lack 18
The Vocalization of Want 19
Verbal Hierarchies and the D.S. 20
Airstream 22
Arms Around the Moon 23
Jadis j'ai cru 24
Moaning at Midnight 27
The Binder, The Looser 29
The Doll's House 31
A Strolling Player 34
Get Out of My Head 38
Trophies on Rage Spikes 40
The First Flaw 42
How Do You Want It to Be 43
Eating Metal, Drinking Gasoline 44

Surveillance and Compliance

Roots of a Revolution 49
Faculty of Reason 53
Heat Loss/ Surveillance in a Blind Eye 56
The Policy of Weakness 59
Are You Musical? 62
A Long Eye 64
Virtual 65
The Year Zero 67
Adjusting the Skill Mix 71

A Brush of Tow	73
Services: Polyptych	75
The American System	85
At Camden Lock	87
Archive of 300 Poems	89
Shiny Circuitry	92
Undercapitalized	94
Over and Over	96
Fragments of the Above	99
Dialogue Poems:	
—The Surface of Denial	101
—Compliance	102
—Part Patterns on Grey Threads	103
Writing on the Paper of You	104
If We Were Immortal, If We Were Not There	105
Objects Under the Voice	107
Acoustic Dynamics	108
Hallucination and mutilation:	
a. Psilocybin	112
b. The Crystalline Structure of North London	114
Personality Inventory January 1988	127

Author's Note

These are two books which originally came out as A4 photocopied things in plastic grips, late wracks of a stage of poetry where people couldn't wait for a publisher and didn't want to compromise with the High Street world. *Sound Surface* was published in 1992, *Surveillance* in 2003, but both belong to a stage of my life when I was working at a telecoms equipment factory somewhere north of the North Circular. Biographically, *Sound Surface* belongs to roughly 1981 and *Surveillance* belongs to 1986, although the composition stretched out over a long period. The urge was always to allow in a wider complex of facts and processes than a straightforward lyric moment. That location in an industrial estate sited near trunk transport routes governed the working week, and much of the poetry is set in leisure time, conveniently demarcated by geography, and spent in Camden Town—a few miles away. Much time has passed, distribution from hand to hand left most people out, it's time to publish them in a technically modern and robust form—and Shearsman have very kindly given me the opportunity to do this.

The original blurb to *Surveillance* says "Although the cycle was begun in 1987, most of these poems were written in 1991 and 1992. 'Services' was written during 1991. 'Heat Loss' and 'The Scream' are rewrites of a poem written in 1980, made in 1988. Work was abandoned in June 1992. In general the cycle took under five years to complete. When I went to work for The Stock Exchange in 1988 I was put on two projects called Surveillance and Compliance.

I rewrote the text in 1995. The 2nd half of the rewrite didn't take place until spring 2001, almost 15 years after the poem began. Cutting some poems in 1995 left a structural gap which had to be filled by new poems. The last rewrite was appallingly depressing to carry out but was demanded by my views of what perfection or finish is. Achievement merges with nonexistence."

The first issues of both books were from 'Five Eyes of Wiwaxia', which in fact was me and a photocopier. Stephen Jay Gould's book *Wonderful Life* described a fossil organism from the Burgess Shale beds which had five eyes—a reconstruction which later methods of getting from flat-packed relics to three-dimensional vividness have swept away. I found the lack of symmetry attractive—different planes of cognitive data failing to map onto each other. Perhaps I was also thinking of 'I've got 96 tears and 96 eyes', a line from 'Human Fly' by The Cramps, itself recalling a certain shot from a certain '50s horror movie.

Acknowledgements

Some of these poems previously appeared in the following magazines and anthologies: 'A Strolling Player' was published in *MEMES* #8; 'Roots of a Revolution' was published in *MEMES* #7; 'Adjusting the Skill Mix' in *InFolio*; 'Services' appeared in *Parataxis* in 1996; 'Heat Loss/Exit Line' appeared in *Garuda* #1; 'Margery Daw', 'Acoustic Dynamics', and 'Over and Over', were published in *Shearsman* 26, 1996, and 'Fragments of the Above' in *Shearsman* 27. 'At Camden Lock' and the 'Dialogue Poems' were published in *Oasis* 69, in 1994. 'Shiny Circuitry' and 'The Policy of Weakness' were published in *Salt* 9, 1996.

'Faculty of Reason' and 'Writing on the Paper of You' appeared in Paul Green's anthology *Ten British Poets* from Spectacular Diseases, in 1993; 'Faculty of Reason' and 'Adjusting the Skill Mix' were published in Iain Sinclair's anthology *Conductors of Chaos* (London: Paladin 1996).

'Roots of a Revolution', 'Heat Loss', 'The Policy of Weakness', 'At Camden Lock', 'Shiny Circuitry', 'Over and Over', 'Fragments of the Above', 'Dialogue Poems' were published in *Anxiety Before Entering a Room. New And Selected Poems* (Cambridge: Salt Publishing, 2001).

My thanks to all the editors involved.

Credits

The information in 'The American System' derives from Derry and Williams's *History of Technology* and Burlingame's *Machines That Built America* (my father's copy). Information used and quoted in 'A Brush of Tow' comes from the *Socialist Review* (February 1992) and *Socialist Worker* (February 1992), both drawing on a book by Peter Linebaugh. In 'The Crystalline Structure of North London', the authorities cited are Jean Calvin (from the *Institutes*), and Alois Riegl (Introduction by Swoboda and Pächt to *The Grammar of Ornament*).

A polyptych is a document of Carolingian estate management, listing all the serfs belonging to the demesne, their obligations, along with lands and other holdings. Not only do they show something of feudal rustic relations, but also they show a very early example of literacy intervening in social relations, and of a new social layer of administrators.

Sound Surface

Suspended Section

"The second feature required for classifying English sounds is the feature called Place."

Imagine
A section through a lodging house.
Tenants and chattels in mid-air
Attitudes struck against a lit decor,
Lying down at night or eating a shared meal.
Tear down the fourth wall,
Open the arch:
Perspective made true by straight walls
Freezing one moment of time
Like a drop caught on the rim.

Bodies caught between the wall and the window
Its sounds stopped and fixed in this
Voices unfold what is known
Over what they know.
The North Circular rolls from A to A
On its banks I'm like the river.
Up beside the hoardings, the blue light
Of a thousand TVs
Stares at the repressed.

Where the spaces designate a set of actions
Stele as incarnation of place: *heroes enkhorioi*
Temples to an indigenous god

Place as the casing of time:
Myth.
Sound from contact of moving planes:
119 Bowes Road.

Hanging Around

I tore it out.
I'm talking about class, the people
You identify with
Who fill your mind with feelings
& you imitate or surpass.
I jacked out. I'm not like the people I grew up with
And I don't do the things I used to do.
The things which entered my eye
Poisoned my heart and
Whatever I hated then has disappeared.
My sight is empty.
I blow down an empty street.

The walls say, you, you
With all the years stored up, the fatigue
All the vice, the disgust with people
All the faults you wanted to unlearn
And all your hatred of the work
And your hatred of the bosses

Are what you have to sell.

I signed on with a wish
Just to lie down on a bed
In a room I paid for
With no-one to watch me.
To do the same thing every day.
Wiping out my self at half past eight
Wiping out every thought at five.
To look in the mirror and see myself
Slack relaxed just
Hanging around.

Meet a New God
Speakers: *the Spirit of Place, Andrew.*

Spi. Scornful, broken, starstruck, bedecked in rags,
    Draped in silence, isolated by shame.
    Passive. Split. Memory wiped. Ranting. Self-denied.
    Fulsome. Lying on filth. Ill. Subservient.
    In these ways you concede to those who hate you
    What you can't bear, the real. Your weakness
    Is the substance of those you, hating, obey.

A. Your father was a lie and your mother was a falsehood
    Your thick beams of illusion pierce living eyes,
    They see their bodies as distortion, they twist
    The human speaking shapes of other people.
    You partition space and fraction sight;
    You run with terror and dominion, you
    Rejoice in buildings and blocking walls.
    You trust in property and scorn living beings.
Spi. You have no safe place to call your own.
A. My view stretches out as far as the wall.
Spi. Your motions reproduce the space we caught you in.
A. My voice takes the real and surpasses it.
Spi. An image formed on dirty waters.
A. Words move at my command, shaking the air.
Spi. Some slurred, some strained, some screamed; some false.
A. Beautiful words could populate this space
Spi. One-ended corrupted by their solitude.
A. Time brought this moment and will take away.
Spi. How many years to climb out of this one?
A. It feeds on itself till mouth and flesh are gone,
    All nature turns on a red axis.
Spi. You rebuild flesh with sick flesh, ideas
    With the data I feed into your senses.
    You're learning the picture others have of you.
A. Every stroke has to be in its place.
    I know your illusions and part their mesh.

Spi. Fantast, you repeat their rejection
    Your own self. Aesthetic procedures
    Write you off as not worth a look.
A. The real is pulverized by words and thoughts.
Spi. A regime of the body adequate for that.
    You can't even do what you could a year ago.
A. By feeling bad I do as you instruct me.
Spi. You're a free agent, feelings are free acts.
A. This devastation is an act of temperament.
Spi. Your illusion is your mutilation, my thoughts
A. Are real in masonry and metal panels
Spi. More solid. You are refuted by what you see.
A. The concentrations of power are too great.
Spi. You are too weak to bring them down
    As they are quick and you are slow
A. My hands are empty. I have no weapon
Spi. Your awareness comprises what's in them.
A. I am ten things at once.
Spi.   Other men's voices.
A. I have such weapons. Time returns again.
Spi. It's likely this mood will be your character,
    Too much in need to receive any help.
A. I deny every word you say.
Spi. By blocks you lost your senses and your insight.
    Indeed this room is what your denial maps.
A. I have no power to affect events.
Spi. This is what you lay out on the market.
A. The complex tasks leave no space for thought.
Spi. Better to work than be yourself and scorned.
    Prescribing your place and acts, your thoughts
    Run like shadows of this solid matter.
A. The poems are thoughts, of higher order.
Spi. Without place or bodies, your conduct is
    To discourse of fantasies with the dead.
A. Since I have no other listeners.
Spi. They hate you in this house, just like
    The people who, not reading, already loathe you.

A.   Five thousand years of perfecting made me.
Spi. A delicate mix of lunacy and pain
A.   My mind is in pieces along broken ground
Spi. The distortion others devised for you
A.   Picking up drops of light to find the way
Spi. Blocked by arrogance and blurred by loathing
A.   Wiping the real to see the future state
Spi. It loses all value in your damaged hardware.
A.   I know what nine words bring the dead to life.
Spi. Jump up on a bench and shout it out
     In the marketplace or in the works canteen.
A.   Stronger voices than mine have stained the air.
Spi. They don't like your squeamish airs and graces.
A.   Art is wealth, I turn the air to gold.
Spi. You adorn what you can't stand to behold.
A.   My faculties are dulled by drudging.
Spi. They ask no better of you, Orphic crow,
     And give you more than you supply to them
A.   The controller of my motions is outside me
Spi. Every limb severed. That's your instrument.
A.   The program is minute and wearisome
Spi. Broader than your gaudy bolts of raving.
     A glass palace of seven stories
A.   Is this a vision?
           Spi. Meet a new god.
A.   Is this our cult?
            Spi. Under trances I send
     Filling null years in these my precincts.
A.   Are you really the voice I made up?
Spi. Your memory. Your construction. Your possession.
A.   I shear the fetters with a blade of flesh.

Circular

A noise comes off the highway
From the metal plates shaking
Numbering the surface of waste energies;
From the hot pipes of the steel throat
In the pinned fabric of motion
The sound rushes across the road shore & rims.

Blast apron
Hard sound over the inadequates
In the pitted surface of the media slew
In the middle of eight million faces.

The motorized column covers its section of loop.
The messages were effaced.
A citadel of numb skin,
Signs arrested
Rooms in the throb of fuel chambers.
The specific metallic signal,
Shivering and blowing away words,
The unwriter of thoughts & patterns.

Along the rims
A certain group moves in to low prices.
They don't understand the signals too well anyway,
It doesn't matter.
You memorized the map that got you here.

No escape by eating transit. A swarm glutted & limed
On foodstuff, stampede of cars
Going round and round between close walls,
Lost migration on the Lost Highway.
One way passage down the throat of insensate words
Laminar sounds peaking to blank uproar
Movements overlaying to a complete circle.
This is the message you were built to hear.
Look for a crack.

Clipping and Shear

In scrolls of solid sound
Crawling through the interdict

At high volumes
of the rage emitter
the distressed equipment shears out other people's feelings.
Blood rush reverb:needle on red one away
from auditory hallucinations.

Code geometry of burnt data.
Cutouts at peaks prolong component life. In shadow pockets
noise becomes signal. In a dark place,
in a drunken stupor, I blank out.
What other people want is beyond me.
I know what she wants and
I put a block on the words and it stops.

Light slanting in a glade
Moving slowly with the hours
Star rise star fall. Where the interdict holds
a snake nailed to a tree lashes and switches but
goes nowhere.
Is it far to go?
Thus what was living
repeats into personality or files
as time seeps out of it
inmota ortonomia.

A whole hoop of nails. Trace every twist:
ornate concentric grams, parallel universes.
Sick oily sweat pouring out of its skin.
Discharge gleam, picture surface.
That's not self-expression.
The integral totality of none such
Impaled on a periodicity of frenzy:
In a maze, an eye which destroys what it looks at.

Consciousness from Lack

This is the history of the jewel.
The killer of eyes freezes time out of sore longing.
My own face and voice,
Flesh peeled away & a flow opens up
along the rail towards
the loved object, where
the stream of presence pours.

The studious exiles refine the topography of dialect
as if they were in the reach of living words
perform the old ballads and dances
as if place poured out of their motions.
detained, ruined, possessed.
Where the pipe was ripped drops fall onto
the tendons of the sun, torn and naked.
The light
the frail protraction forms images from
whatever impinges penetrates corrupts,
grains the extended flaw.
The freezing of time—
the thousand sips of false memory.
Glisten of
protective fluid forming around the wound.

I spent my childhood trying to get back home

introversion melancholia formalism.

The Vocalization of Want

Words flow and I ask who controls them.
Their tint is that of whoever is near.
Where once there was an embrace
Space bursting from around a loved body
To wrap and cherish and relieve

is a scream torn from my lips.
mouthfuls spat out in a retch, I'm starving.
I'm eating and I can't swallow
I'm gibbering and I can't form a word
the sound is the mutilation of that embrace
the flexible limbs of solitude
outlining mine.
Longing has taken my appetite.

Fragments in their thousands roam the streets.
A generation of spectres repairing their prisons
taking hoardings for their skin
walking along the ballast
singing what the train sings
The mechanized exit goes on and on.
what passes through the wail is destroyed.

The crack in the wall; the worn mouth.
The ray slitting a thick slab of anxiety.
Language seeping through the zone of suppression
   …denatured. Wavelengths altered.
A pattern emerges from loss of signal,
fluids are seeping across a line of division.

The hand which wounds is the hand which heals.
ah! it is made bright, it is wrapped up for the slaughter.
& that hand wires the circuits of illusion

Verbal Hierarchies and the D.S.

Plants on the windowsill.
They turned us over
Seven am.
How they spoke to us
Get up get your strides on
And mocking my household goods
How they spoke to Mister the Landlord, who let them in
Those lickspittles in blue know who owns the law.
Gangster slang and Official English,
Barks of command or else treacly smears and sirs.
You could tell how much we're each worth
With your eyes closed.
They know class the way their dogs know who they can bite.
A symbolic system so beautifully held in mind
As if by piss on the boundary lines.
What you think is just the echo of what's said to you.

A drug, a sleepy dust
What they put naughty children to bed with in Cyprus,
Banned because it makes people happy and so
Stops them working hard. I put it to you
Justice doesn't come into it
You just want us to be unhappy
And I'm doing what you want.
Unhappiness makes one unable to learn or to act or to work,
Thus denying revenues to the State.
The streets, sir, make people find a place to hide.

Scott went to live on someone else's floor.
Owes the State 297 pounds at three pounds a month.
The Government can wait. Knowing what people have.
Like winter, they're long creditors.
His factory laid him off.
They had no more steel left, strike in force.
He'll get the dole could be

Or thirteen pounds benefit. Held down by silks
Crime slips away, who caused who
Suffering? Property's in paper. Learnt by dogs.

Airstream

The pales set too close
cause the man of leisure
pacing a slatted bar of open space
to waste away.
The body eroded by commands
broken motions of a barred landscape
Spaziergang.

I cut a pouch in the city fabric
to shelter in from peering eyes.
A skin to close upon the sore.
So many paces across; an arm's span in the plumb-line.
Wave breaks, shaking volumes
a sound specific to each space.
Each body gives off a local music,
Take sounding. The ring distributes itself in words

Arms around the Moon

a vain shape in my arms.
the rain gathering in the hollows & impact holes forms pictures.
my picture forming in the bright eyes without memory.
the vacant lots flourish green & wanton.

the swept blade answerable to the air through which it moves
The leaf spread to the sunlight it will catch
The body answerable to its like.
Waiting for heat

when the chain of knowledge parts.
when the memory falls silent:
when the senses refrain from their falsehood.
in the air my arms close around and push away.

Strike up! buried motion
in eye and hand and waist
separated from the absent music
of the musicians in painted clothes.
beams pick up lapses of body's slow swim.
Embrace the moon after its journey,
the light extenuated by longing,
the nimble cadences like bat's wings and moths.

Jadis j'ai cru

I once believed
We could make our home where in the large rooms
A smell of wax and flowers would fill the air
And, where music trembles and disappears
Along rolls of time cooped in the wood
You would have your wish.
Each word I hear slips
From those rooms, I know by its
Acoustics; as fallen stones prove by curve and working
To be heaven's rooftiles slid during a storm.
The words of poems dapple a vanished whole. A straight cadence
Lifted from the stream of presence.
Space bursts from around your body, close to you
Is everything I imagine or desire.

Out of thin air a voice composes
A glass palace of seven stories in a wet meadow
Of flowers scattered in flecks of blue and red
As if the callous tossing wind had seen a carpet pattern,
And grasses lush and springy to the foot,
This side of bog but sopping bright awash in Spring, poured
By a river of sweet water where we swim
Down walls between blue rock falls
Or up still green-padded creeks snagged by willows,
Or across broad flat reaches to the islands;
Conducted in channels of human art,
Through mirrors of trees bowed by weight of apples,
Where the slow hum of wasps slows to show
The thief nuzzling at the sun in the flesh.
Below, winding off the mush of pulpy apples,
Split, slackened, soil-crusted, on the turn,
A heady smell reminds me of coarse strong drink.

I went across the river

As day inclines and breaks in colours
an claidheamh soluis
The reddish sword of light
Catches on the webs and fine moisture of the meadow
Walking along the tips of grass-blades and clovers
Where gossamer or rain or floss or first dew
Twine a net of reflecting surface
It shimmers in darts where the wind moves along it, refracts,
And the sword
Writes a broad shining track.
The attendants slight the palace of the day
To draw the groundplan of the fort of night.
On the municipal playing field
Just where the Wood Brook enters the town
Walking along light threads
I fold up my cloak of lies; slight breaths
Falling like petals from the heady inane.
I imagine what I lack.

Night wears its tints through, another day wipes dry
The visible from the thorough vapours of darkness.
Falling mingling with the sunlight we hear
The second language, not that
Which changes with the nations and the coasts
And sullies with each fleck of distance and matter,
And dies as its wave form dissipates, instead that other
Which is universal and immense and
Is spoken by the heart, audible
In summers and on mountains and by moonlight.
What is to fire as fire to wood?
Or what colour is the horse of air
Which carries birds in the direction of our longing;
I found its track in ashes and ruins
Whether
In some Northumbrian love song like 'I drew my ship'
Or in an Appalachian ballad dubbed from an old 78
Rustic chivalry slowly set out in courtly state

To adorn the beauty of a farm girl
Or at the named moment
When patterns overlay and match
In a woman's face turned towards me.
It's just an old song I misremembered.

A span out of the fundamental structure of space.
As during exile
As a child who had to live in homesickness
My voice was part of what I had lost and I
Froze it to keep that sound from contagion
Now silence is my part but I still remember
The house of large rooms.
My family appeared by intermittence, light
Shone right through it when it was there.
I kept faith in carceral conditions.
Ruled by an idea at nine years old
I learnt then how to be an artist,
Kept warm by the intangible and
Fed sleek and fat by the unreachable.

Split between two places I am half now
Of what you want to possess
You seize on my intermittence
And I can't paint across the gaps
I can't build that house.

Moaning at Midnight

In the front room above the North Circular
Live Barry and Charlie, gay as sunshine
Buried under noise.
At midnight when the road is calmer
And its load of memory fades into a yellow quietus
And the branch line trains grow rare
I hear the bed next door creaking. Low moans.
Physical theatre. For this they tolerate each other.
For this they infect each other.
Five feet one
Ugly as sin
Unskilled labourers
TV versus traffic noise
Middle-aged cough, at nights: a broken shaft
Into a pit of refuse.
Irish dialect, Scots dialect. Nothing to say.
Semi-employed immigrants. Nowhere to go.
They will die in decaying property. In Iran
They kill such people; here they eat themselves away.

that Ireland might be free
strong men ranting the night away
in song and strong drink
wild geese longing for green dewy dells.
Wherever you want to live
I don't see any signs of motion.
Wherever your songs are
You're right here in our backyard.
Whatever ancestors you commemorate
Your blood line ends here. Smeared on the road.
Last glimpses of imagined home, visible
In alcohol. Miraculous.

Just a few feet away
 This lorn lover kicks unruffled sheets

Not Platonic but alone.
Radio Desire flows over the soft airsea
Like flakes marbling a deep mill pool
How can I go on living like this?
Who could I share it with?
500 yards away
Like a fox snuffling the vocal ground to trail another fox,
a streak of signs that bind and wind in,
The moon dips long white legs along the river reach;
I heard it call my name.
Where does my country lie
Or what ship could draw up to take me there.

The Binder, The Looser

I call by name, I petition
The attendant of procurement,
Who is one half soft & white & one blue and dead,
the one who writes down the names of lovers
and throws them, in black foam
Over flowing white weeds, in the river.
The one who sits by the well. I tender a contract. The one who
Draws silver down from the moon
And maims whatever she finds too beautiful:
Canidia. I lay down a bar of gold, I lay down a bar of iron.
Let that beautiful woman want me. Let her burn up for lack of me
Let her eyes grow dim until she sees me
Let her pine away for lack of me. Into her white flesh
Into her fierce wishes
Let my love reach like blood.
Let my face form on every still water, my voice
In every breeze that blows.
I go into the open field
I go into the meadow uncut by blade of metal
I stand in the sweet and light-shaken water
I call her name
What she wishes, let it be destroyed.
Who she loves, let him be forgotten.
Where she is, let it vanish until distance is within my reach.

And the enchantress reads the scroll of lead
Which draws a line around my body
Which couples me with the darkness and calls down that solitude
Where my voice is like ten dogs wrangling
And thoughts wisp away before an image forms.
My limbs dissolve from around my wish.
She who draws down the moon into wan waters
Piles up the bones of my love
Beside the fountain of my words.
Let not a chime the nightly hours sing,

Let not the lyric lark salute the day
Nor Philomela tune the sad dark away;
Canidia still draws on.

The Doll's House

We make a picture to distract our weary hours.
In the picture a mother in the petals of light
makes the doll out of flowers.
"Hazel for wisdom, lilies for your dress.
Watercress for your growth, oak for your lifespan.
Clover for the couch of pride, heartsease for your darks.
For your wine, the taut and velvet grape,
Cherries for your cheeks, ashwood for your bones.
A bower of hawthorn to be your home."

keeping odd house
in joints of words and beams of fancies

we make a home of rain and ditches
we furnish a board with pots and dishes
make a household of nails and blood
wear a dress of furs and masks
boil a kettle of bones and flesh

In the room full of clothes and heads
you make a doll with my shape and teach it manners
I make a doll with your shape and call it Columbine

the two dolls fight and one dies
it eats the other's body and has two faces
two impulses jerk its limbs this way and that
we fight over the doll
draw boundaries on its skin.
With kitchen knives I cut the face I want to see
you stretch a skin over it. A strip of sores and chaps and flaws.
Come deck my body in the finest array
A mouth scraped in the roiled earth: clay grin
over teeth of sett & flint & brickbats.
We teach it rigmarole and paraphrase

It says "Serve the people. Red axis threads all nature.
Iron rescues captive eyes. Mend and scour the ditches."

fighting over the doorway, fighting over the script
fighting over the rules of the game
fighting over the truth. fighting for control.

one second of harmony
our breaths falling as gold to the floor
gold drops, speckle flour, gold puddles, spills
sighs like fine-wrought S's and strapwork
gold steam on the window

The doll says
"Sometimes I have a nickel, sometimes I have a dime".

a hand draws lines in the waste ground
and the earth starts up
working in a warm place beneath a folded cloth
the brim of the standing water turns to skin
uncoiled wire turns to nerves
a bird's beak to be its voice
it says "Is she white as milk and soft as silk
Is he strong to guard and shelter?"
light a fire of tallow to give it go
a dredge of flour to make it neat
the exercise called tumbledown teeter
rust turns to blood and colours the skin warm
"what does this taste like
what place is this, what rain"
It has joy in running, in the windrush
Eyes move to trace the green mill of sap
There are hands to grab and tell the mint of noon.
Aloud it cried
To see the daylight disappear,
And feel its eyes turn back to water.

when soul and body part
I can't move, when I speak the doll's lips move
You can't stand up, fighting for control
in our house. I move my arm and yours moves,
You shape a thought and I think it.

a magpie lighting on bright eyes, a quick mouth
she is dainty, she is choice
she must have her wish. Snipping and stitching
pinning it up in the pattern she would want:
trick it out in panes of red and yellow, throw it on the floor.
Aroused and frustrated
she tries to realize the idea.
organs piled in the kitchen.
nip its bones apart to pick their marrow,
cut it in stars and dredge it with white meal.
its skin comes away. its tongue comes right out.
a hole in its forehead to take the words out.
it's nothing like.
Contrary doll that will not dance or sing
Or set out bricks in coves and rooms.
She is dull, she is listless.
Dress it up and put it away.

A strolling player

the stage flats have been rolled up
the space has disappeared.
the metaphors ornament what they can't reveal
The shapeshifter unfolds and the mirror dispels him face by face
My flocks drift towards unreal pastures. A poet or a prince of men
Sends his columns towards the unknown river. A sacrifice.
Love and work make up a man.
a life that could be seen by any passer-by
without the sense of having no right and being stripped of honours
Those two things I dream about, since I can't do those things
I can't react, I can't conceal, I can't amputate and I can't feel
I can't mean, I can't persuade, I can't destroy and I can't use.
I can't touch you. I can't see you. I don't need you and I don't love you
Because I'm not part of the life I wanted to lead
because I don't need what I can't use
because my lips won't obey my brain
nor will what's in my head take shape
nothing stands still
a thousand ideas flash up and rush away

this can't be pain
I can't tell you apart from me
this can't be pain
ten thousand bright flakes
I can't even find out where it is

Everything I say ceases to be true

I can't take two steps

Your absence cannot take from me what is mine:
You were a glance of a whole whose shape was outside geometry
Your desertion
Cannot veil the midnight or make the tides of Saturn more leaden
Or make the rivers flow away more quickly

Or ruin the solitudes under flocks of birds with human voices.
My holdings
Lie across the river.

These magnificent things I have lost.
A sacrifice. For no reason just as a gesture of wealth
A ceremonial pretence.
I throw my life away
As if I had ever owned anything except poems
As if I had the disposition of this estate
From one institution to another.

Fine words are cheap and yet don't sell.
Go to the factory, lay down your thoughts at the gate
Do the work that's always the same
Until you shed your flightiness, become durable and steady.
I do what a million men have done
And what a million men do, I do.
I repeat ten thousand times
What I never believed in the first place.
Their commands are stable while I am inconstant:
Too many ideas, just learn how to work.

Trying to be other than what I am.
Ah, those thoughts of other people.
If willingness to help and affection answer for a lot
At work
Antipathy and wet disgust count for more.
I'm not the same as them
Yet every drop of rotting cell
Stains me and finds its brother here.
I go there willingly. Drained shapes,
Move across the eye, the eye moves the inner shadows.
I bite on nothing; try to hold my breath all day.
I drink water from another's lips,
Grow my tendrils in foul air.
I stoop under the prevailing Time,
Cherish words and illusions under class war.

Where is love?
I smile to show I'm clean inside
But the smile is nervous and ragged.
Do I love you in the hot dead cinema?
Two hours of no future.
Do I love you at work?
I walk along corridors past live exchange racks, open backed
Wires like a brain.
I make jokes and tension gives like a hawser spat on,
I wipe my brain down to earn a living
In the Switching and Main Exchange Division.
I get less conscious as I repeat, and more skilled.
Do I use my leisure hours to love you?
In the evenings the figures pass before me
Softened like ink washing away in rain
Between five and eight.
I can't see images, I dream in figures.
What else is there in me?
What can I love with?

I try to capture the minutiae of the zone
People walk by with their severed faculties
Hanging out of their skins by veins without walls
And I can't help. They're part of a society which doesn't exist
And I can't dream it up. I try to fit
The hundred loops on the hundred hooks.
I deny and deny and can't choose but to
Live as I'm told. What happens to them
Happens to me. I carry the money home.

He puts his arms around her
And she sees a picture of his weakness
She kisses him
And he subtracts the dead hours
They make something that never was before
And see it can't sustain human life.
He feels comfort and consolation

And she finishes the reckoning.
As they cling together, the horizon filling their arms
Their senses sharpen to the final pitch
And what they hear tears them apart.
Revenge and guilt tinge the crack of light
Vision descends burns strikes them with shame.

You tear me to shreds,
An airy man, a handful of cloud.
You don't want anything out of books;
You ask me why I've got no career.
Rich on words mope in penury
sordid and exalted
rhetor's splendour lofting over back streets and piles of waste
expound and posture unsure of any rank
writing a book to possess what's in it.

Who reaches the peak of years of unhappiness
Lives in a vision for a few months
Then realizes that the means of winning the new life
Could only be years of happiness
Gleaming out from eye and step and voice;
And from the heights
Sees Time melt shackles to forge chains
Which is called, learning;
And a warrior cutting the water with a knife
Which is called: healing.

I watch my projects fall in ruins
Buildings falling out of the sky in rubble
Ideas breaking up into stubs and slurs.
I watch the spectacle for hours
Pictures falling past my eyes in streams.
When the basic equipment is corrupt
Each shape repeats,
The flesh breeding true after its kind.
So, this is permanent.

Get Out of My Head

To walk around and to be possessed
To have a sexual being and to be possessed, to hear words
And be instructed, to need money
And to be sold.
To have your own feelings which occupy people
And crave for compliance.
To be seen by hourly eyes as services
Met or due; disparaged.
To covet feelings you can't acquire: luxury objects
Under a deep gloss.

Developing the mysteries of mise-en-scene,
she is chiding the failed evening
where you were cold and pessimistic,
sordid and without vigour.
She has a vision which demands compliance,
I have anxiety which pores over fine detail.
To elaborate the very scene
And employ someone else for the responses;
To improvise
And be cut down.
To glow in a display window, to be offered for,
And be sold for menial work. This is the age of discernment.

A thousand failed tests
projected into the unconscious.
I read my wages slip, devise
A real self. Get out of my head.

Depression is the Other's reality at point of sale,
the exaction of the skill-intensive economy.
In the plate-glass city,
after its spirals of refinement,
you look at models of feeling and moving
Like pictures being projected in your room.

It's your name on the files at the DHSS,
The exams putting a value on your brain,
the clear notions of the panel.
It's a rest from sexual competition:
not desiring what is desirable; out of
The struggle for domestic power,
Where acquiring someone is like shopping
& unhappy people realize the program of unhappiness.
You lie down on a velvet case and wide-smile.

Harsh reflexive agents
We wait for the big concerns, the West End frontages,
The opera house, to buy us in. Precious skin
Displayed among crystal and marble.
For you I'm inadequate
Though you're my ideal. Get out of my head.

Trophies on Rage Spikes

I memorized their lies
I memorized their lines

The loathing I feel for other people
Causes the loathing they feel for me
Which is why
There is no more because

Violence repressed, back
Realized in theory
Destroys the surface of the world
Solid blocks of denial crushing each object,
Flesh drawn out by force.

Out of reach
The shining surface
Mocking screen. psychotic mirror.
No input. No pain. Blood beating in pulse.

I perceive the world
As if giving way to a stronger enemy
Prone
My face ground into the grill he carved. Sign bearer.
Ritual scripts enacted
Pools of blood and bones, burn over
The surface of perception;
grande ligne climax
A desert of concrete and tarmac. Fixed by fire.

Magazines like freezers
A pink thigh eight feet wide above the soft shoulder.
Media lies like successful
Mutilations, joints hung up in the
Smoke of small burning bones,
Continue our false consciousness.

Distortion graved by rage.
Social being as twenty facets of hatred on an eye,
Self as mirror of that lens.
Dress of putrescing skin, calcined pipes and soft parts.
Big screen: body count.
Speaking flaw: I hate your insides. Speech ban.
A sound that dissolves sound.

Dream up monsters
Make them into behaviour machines.
Crush overwrite cancel other people's feelings.

The First Flaw

Oars, willows, sedge, waterfowl. No names.
Cut the first tree for the first pile of the first dock,
Waiting for the first ship ever to sheer into the Medway,
A Dutch crew with a cargo of nettles and vetch.
No lighters, clear her by wading out across the beach.
Beach the keelless, wicker-and-skins, local trade.
Broad fairways pointed to these marshes and low clay hills
And the people built the city they imagined
And became the people the City imagined.

Kent: the edge (*Kante*), face towards Europe
And where civilization comes from. Finery and treason.
Thieves picking the loads, buyers and royal officers,
Speculators, hanging around the wharves and hutments.

Ask why this city works the way it does
Why the acts of other people make you act this way,
Why the parting of space set out these emotions, how
They redraw that order every time a new street goes up.
You'd have to start by razing the city. Get set by razing the people.
Clear zones new intakes
A thousand patterns for a new way of things
Each one corrupted by the people who learn it.

Dig to the first stratum. Somebody lied.

How Do You Want It to Be

We can't vote, they took us off.
Householder struck us off the register, so
If we wanted to prove we lived anywhere
It couldn't be proved
And he has no relationship with us.
No rent-book no taxes no rights,
The papers only work one way: what you feel
Isn't legally true.
As they do, with transients in lodging-houses,
Dropping them off so they can't even vote,
As if what they wanted could be had.
As if this city belonged to the people in it.

Vague drifters
Even the walls can't keep from fading out
Effaced speech. Way states who never arrived.

What I wanted to say remains unsaid
What I hate remains vertical

I don't have a home
because I can't afford to buy one
But I voted for Ken Livingstone to run London.

Eating Metal, Drinking Gasoline

Mouth like a power saw biting lines in metal
bright wake tore through the heart of steel sheeting
heart like railroad steel

I pick up the forces and make them my own

Listen for the numbers.
Buried star rings out throb-field. Masses shake out along its ridges, shun
        blanks & troughs.
Vortex carving holes in the solid urban fabric
rush gulleys. power scars. combustion scours.
Inhuman calls metering me.
verberación del ayer
Spatter and blare. Inside the sound. Big bad beat.
Shooting on rails in the second geography of signals
Crowds rushing high on chemotactics
like termites to sugar.

Draw the gram out on paper, cut it in glass. Catch it in the black silver.
Wave-beat of crowds hollows buildings, damages objects into shape
between the valleys of the Lee and the Fleet.
On the ridges, there you feel high.
Watch the vibrations on the Thames. Drowned offerings strophe us,
Riverbed Triads. Crab ooze cynghanedd.
Numb velocity
Craving matter
To realize itself in. Each body
A mouth for the shriek searching.
Sex class money. Religion hatred rock and roll.

What city
Erects a monument to the woman who burnt it down?
Celtic queen whetting stone axle-blades
under granite lungs of stallions
At the river's edge in touch with ash-layer.

Burning over
The port where the slaves were embarked,
Migrants to who knows what distant town,
Modernized
Neck-fettered, writing hung around their collar,
As the land registry marks the estates for the Romans;
I record two millennia of lies
And prepare my own registries.

hallucinate the city & hallucinate its absence
& hallucinate it and deface the stolen image
and at last come to understand the Outer
by modelling and appropriation.
I eat the city.

'74
I was a metal worker
There in Loughborough
Making steel doors: gates
In unnamed space. Ripsaws & hammers & grinders
Eating my way through shiny oxidized laminae.
Red and green skeins of surface crystals,
Musk & cinnamon from burnt wood beneath the drill-bit,
Two twirls of smoke & bit-waste.
Give it some hammer.
Straight edges hanging in empty air.
I made parts of: prisons, asylums, a monastery.
I bow to the superior technology. I blank out to analyse the machines.

Surveillance and Compliance

"I am with all the wild Irish at the same point I am with bears and bandogs when I see them fight; so that they fight earnestly indeed and tug the other well, I care not who have the worst."
—Lord Justice Arnold to Lord Cecil, letter, January 1565

"Do not go to the soothsayers and lying Chaldaeans, who are in the house of darkness. Do not eat or drink at the house of the twelve doors."
—Gnostic Scriptures

"(T)he maxim being infallible that all kingdoms must be preserved by the same means by which they were first gained"
—Fynes Moryson, *Itinerary*

"Chi Hsing-Tzu was training a fighting-cock for the king. After ten days the king asked, 'Is the cock ready?'

'Not yet', says the trainer. 'It is full of fire and arrogance.' Ten days the king comes to enquire again. 'It is still not ready. The sight of its rivals still excites it.' Ten days later the same question. 'It has not yet rid itself of its angry stares and excessive ardour'.

Ten days later the trainer at last announces 'Now we are ready! The crowing of the other cocks leaves it impassive. Before its foes, it is as if it was made of wood. Its inner strength is such that its opponents dare not defy it. They take one look and run away.'"
—Zhuang Dze, xix, 8, translated Simon Leys

Roots of a Revolution

In the stasis of fearful energies I flip out unconscious
Twenty thousand people fired and I've made a career.

A head stream of dark air. The world buckles
We represent it, gritting our teeth and closing our eyes.
Some people can't even see it and
Ah! we see every trait!
Why the ships cross the seas
Why the reactors burn
Why the shortages and what shapes the flesh is worn into.
We see a sense that marshals events
From the pipes of Siberian gas
To the waiting lumber of Brazil
From the cracking vapour of the refineries
To the trays of goods hawked in the supermarkets.

Look traveller at this site
An island on the edge of the ocean waste
Wharf space plus warehouses plus finishing shops
They live by buying and selling each other.

A comb of scant living spaces; the metaphor
Of a ship: a rope's end and cramped berth on
A trading venture. Sailors overseeing slaves
And officers sailors. Every inch reckoned and
Bodies fitting in those inches. Movement banned.
Fingering the trade goods down in the hulk.

Why are the crowds running in the streets?
A fit has afflicted the people of the island
They stand out on the moor in thousands
Tearing at their heads till the blood flows and tearing,
Expounding Scripture and chanting sales slogans
Mumbling broad paternosters and thieves' rigmaroles

Imitating a leader as he barks like a dog,
Focuses on thin air, washes water with clay,
Scribbles copies of till rolls on waste paper,
Eats leaves, wearing pans tied to his wrists,
Clutches bundles of rags and pours lye on scabs.
Pressing together till the middle is crushed,
The envelope of flesh overflows.
A red dragon lashes among the crowds,
Ten thousand flour weevils move in step behind a leader,
A headless horse gallops over the moor,
Its body is fleshed and ribbed with our mania,
Racing in a sweat to turn a mill
It breaks up our homes.
Thousands of pilgrims are selling their houses
They are rushing south and tearing away north
And none could say where he was going to.

The factories are empty and the streets
Are full of sleeping people.
Simply that their last inch was stripped.
Their minds revert to the other space, the boundless featureless.

Goods piling up in the halls, the lorries
Never pulling out. Too much inventory.
The drivers cold with standing, drifting
In and out the office. All out of destinations.
We serve as many as will
Whoever they are, boys,
They won't take our gear,
Their will is free where relationship is compulsion,
Whatever's in their homes
It's foreign or they don't have no homes.
Rig your sails by the weather.
Cut your prices, take in your throat.

Quick capers tow row a brave cotillion
Danced to a far spectator

Somewhere in EC2, or in a Washington front office
Tossing hands to my head with trained gestures
Dwarfed by remoteness
Please please please

I count timings and outputs
A footsoldier of the New Right
A Black Guard of the repressive revolution
A shantyman of the speedup on the line
Marshal of group motion.
Enforcing the new norms. Locating the waste
To pare off, even be it of organic form,
In two shoes. Don't you understand
If you can make the speed
You don't have to die?
There is no because in group illusion
It's an outburst of hatred, a communal violence,
It's like religion it's like war. A shared game,
A ritual excitement, under drums and herbs.

Why are people dying in the streets
It's part of the price mechanism,
As an expression of human wishes
Whose aggregate is you die in the markless space.
It's part of the sin mechanism
It's an organ of State.
The tall buildings are empty;
Waste under the arches and in the underpass.

A fit that drove me for those years
Like burning ashes in my hand.
Ask what skills I mastered,
Precise knowledge modelling the universe.
Ask, what passions worked me,
What kind of man was this and what faith this was,
What fits and appetites in my body:
This dream—winch the norms up.

The screw turns another notch. My arms knot and rip.
My mind beaten soft.
I wiped my ideas, slept
Beneath my lathe. I wanted to get the goods out the door
And keep the factories open and
I cut the water with a knife.

Tell me I was never there
Tell me my awareness is provincial errors
Tell me human awareness is unwarrantable
Tell me I wasn't part of the group I belonged to for nine years
Tell me I wished for this to happen
Tell me not to empathize.
Rationalize my words
Rationalize my memories and my emotions
Rationalize the society I belonged to.
Illuminate, turn, and erase.

The Faculty of Reason

You reach the door of the lit room
You wring your hands and stand at a loss
They won't let you in their room
You picture the clean worked objects in there
They won't let you use their words.

They own these spaces
Whose cleanness is the missing certain kinds of people
Their doors are stronger than your hands that beat and talk.
Flow segmented neatly between closed doors, bodies
Snapped in a grid of checkpoints &
They know where you are
They know you by the way you string thoughts together
You flutter your hands and bring out
Objectless words

Those machines just cost too much to have
Fools snatching at their switches
Grades and taunts rehearse your future part,
These things a child foresees
Dismay young reason. Those crises
Of teasing weren't for play, you saw your face
Coming back to you with holes running over it
In the place of silence and rejection.
The game of shutting people out was practice
For an economic system. A group exercise.
You were defiant when alone
Taking dreams and rags as your lot.
When you're outside security gates
Clutching a paper biography
Like the blue tag clipped in a cow's ear
You make Personality as sweet babble,
You use astrology to reclaim control.

You can still buy a human being today
And the ones not are littering our streets.
Public space. No-one's. Not cleaned.

You come out of the hospital and
madness was just a protective screen
against the Reason which marks you in your segment.
This society's just too hard to join.
On the penitential island
Now that four walls and a fire are beyond price
the whole outdoors is cold and broad to use as Punishment
For those who wander.

Hewed proscenium shelters raggle taggle;
arcuate bastion waiting for sham guns,
Stormed and four ways slighted by troops of air
in accoutrements of stray wool, governed by loose music.
sham ruined household strewn in clouts and cans.
Drink for cloth and bags for pans.
Why, with tools & teck they could have walls on four sides of you.
With teamwork & straightedges they could stuff every chink.
Blow, blow, is the verdict.
The creature is suited to its place.

In the walls of ceramics banded with fat and gold
cameras have recorded wealth and family and taste,
the defences of the skin denying its nature
a frozen body in a symmetrical grid.
The household made of organized knowledge
the dense chancery
of ownership marks and price data behind
gull's wing gates, swept and polished as if whetted,
where the segments part and are sealed.
the light of tempered judgement falls
through ionized constant air, through
glass roofs with their rolling metal blinds,
onto a dove grey anode finish,

onto capital asset chattels.
They judge you by your shoes then judge you by your words

As I do. The seekers of lost knowledge
recite sutras and oracles, read from the flying roll
To tell lies about Destiny and Self.
Woman, don't you throw a lot on me
Nor cast up the King of Babylon
Nor make your arrows bright at the head of two ways,
In an empty place where way there is none.
What is flows from what was,
You erase that memory which
Tells us where you are. You build an astral myth
Where rays ripple over you, prove everyone wrong
And find yourself all out and down.
You believe the things they taught you,
You drill gaps in your consciousness, whispers
Sifting through the perforations
bring you news from another world.
That's your house isn't it

You lose your reason because they own the land.
Because of what you are
Because of what you did
They won't let you in their room. You can't say what's square.
Those whose anxiety was too great
To be used as the belt which drives them
won't be made to obey for anything.

They don't even want your obedience.
They're upping the output norms,
Sending the lines offshore, tearing off the payrolls
And asking for maths.
The factories are closing and there aren't
Even yards you could sweep out
Or pallets you could stack.

Heat Loss/surveillance in a blind eye

testing a frame's
figure of
light or confinement
ripping sensation from the head,
the eye in retaliation
is truly a hole in the skin, a flaw
tending to heal over

tapping out the perimeter
the cipher covers the small rectangle
within the larger rectangle;
one of paper one of masonry
scan and retrace
the free zones of sight
gored by the factory buildings
property in contest
reaching out around the physical sheath:
I am what I see.

A quarter-mile of dead windows

I can't span those vaults
stretched by a firm and fiery gaze
where blue-white birds would fly, and we with them.

My eye crosses to the opposite blank façade
and sees another bored eye staring out at me
as I sit for years without moving
frustrated motion frays the boundary of order
Birds sheer and scream
Aeons of energy
Crackling blue where the air touches them
haemorrhage in blue outline
held breath of sonic assassin,
telescopic sights deleting

whatever they pick out, cirque of darkness.
I gaze across at them
hallucinated and numb.

in the morning I wake

And do not wake
depression closes it all out.
dead senses heat seal: a ravelin
raised on optic principles.
the quadrants of light slighted

When rage is denied
to want a place destroyed
see it disappear from under you
as you go there every day
the rage of others caught it
Nice town. Burn real pretty.

Watching my self elapse
in long roaming shapes,
probing
the boundary where time leaves flesh:
red on black; bone dice, spectre chattering numbers,
drinking mercury and smoking strips of fire,
the turn of a card
wipes out my time.
officer buying up fifty years of debts
takes your paper off the market.
A name expired,
signal eddy of dying circuit chips
smeared on hardtop
response curve neatly terminated in curtain sheer.
Work it off

Beneath, the shop floor.
stasis wrench numb order

grinding of energies
almost solidified by monotony
crimped and implemented
locked on target

Furtive and silent
terrorized by the shouting voices
furtive and tranquil
a door breaks contact and sound
Out of the path of the Powers
writhing in recoil
turn and turn

Don't make me go out there.

Sodden with rancour
In a hired room
waiting for my head to clear.
Watching the light travel across the window

I crossed the river, lay me down to sleep.
When I woke up there was shackles on my feet.
Each separate limb caught in a chain
And on each link a letter of my name.

I crossed the river, lay me down to sleep
And in that sleep I heard sweet strains of music.

The Policy of Weakness

You get the picture, a china jug in 17 pieces, cell and cowl,
slashed fuel lines, frost on the can, desertification,
setting fires under water, stilled flattened framed, yes we see.
Put a frame round it. Mutilate it. Rant and rail.

When I first met Mark, he said I needed a piss
in a pub by Euston Square, a bag of white stuff
was behind the knuckle of the pipe that made me
blush to my collarbones. Thousand mile stare. So
I came back to this ruin of ruinous livelihood.

Midnight on the wharf of the glass sea, rain on the leaves of the summer
    trees
The infrared stores of the stacked bricks wash through the billows of rain
enclosed space
modulated by four people
around a tumbledown room near the multiplex of railway tracks
as the night sets sail from the green shores of the Grand Union Canal

Chill swirrs from the blue interiors of foliage
Two talkers, high on ideas.
How false I feel smothered in the skirts of your
big opulent durable feelings, your
so fluent and false intuitions of Being
setting sexual lures. Mark yarns about dealing in Liverpool. While I

dans les plâtras de mes combinaisons écroulées
the spinner of a formal span that rots in neglect and darkness
crushing dust into stone and flesh into dust!
sumptuous flourishing piers, on paper only,
tender skin ridged with swelling and fever.
Decidedly my enterprise is ready for commissions
I have no debts no stock and no policy.
If there is leisure one has to do things without motive.

In a stupor straining to measure what to conform to
in the room but not in the script, smiling
vague and like a viper in shock
I pour every drop into the broken cup

She was a pilgrim on the Bad Drug Way from Keele to Camden,
she wants to be a teacher and they won't let her near their kids
she wants to be a faith healer and cuts reason away
some anecdote about psilocybin, hospital, and lung damage
she's got five voices coming out of her head and
she is filled with yearning by my new Soho haircut

a mirror for demons, a snapshot of depth
the gaze which captures and reads
uncovered surfaces could find out my weakness or
acquire personality traits by imitation
I can't read the signature of these events
in the picture of desire fulfilled and lofty souls that
tell me what controls me and
try to scoop me up like ice cream. Smooth swatches,
sex talk, display, blinding glint of words, it's
the strong against the weak.

After scenographic shimmering floods of anxiety
the act of identification caught and cut into frames,
proteins freeze as glass. Passionate
white powder. A shocked hurt thing that turns and turns
and has no body
hand on mouth choking on involuntary knowledge
faced with the music but not rising to dance
A lyric poem without a hero who in a clean room
opens the filters to engorge the objects of
long persistence and toxic effect
on frail native tissue. How much I admire
the pylon throb of your feelings in which I deploy
mimic response. You mistake my silence and apathy for
sweetness of character. I rise to go.

Streets hosed with hissing yellow light.
Planning Monday's shift in my head.
Singular matrix error at hex address 74B791
No response from logical unit 128
Pictures going down the data line to Harlow
through stages and under the earth.
Do you know what a singular matrix might be, Ruth?
Do you think two geometries might not fit and engage
gushing down the dark channels of this summer night

Are You Musical?

On the way there, I make the romances
stepping scanning a train
of very fast movements
simultaneously in seven planes,
running on two screens; freeze frame;
slowed up; colour bleached; cut to the music.
Women are set out in patterns round a room
Dazzle unravels at the height of eyes and ears
I fall through North London like a knife through water
to seize heat in my hands;
adorned for violence and finesse.

Water of the stars that frighten,
signed sound from a deformed bell
topologically read by the scanning of numbers
holding something underneath my tongue
like 400 hours of some undenting folk genre
quivering between its limits to score
a petty geology.
If this is your self, walk around in it then.
A snake with cloth skin, a gestural aura
discrepant with the physical goods.
A stable daze. Signals trapped in pipes.

Blossoming cascade of improvisation, divine
foregrounding of rules that makes error
a new sequence and transgression
the sparse matrix of a new anatomy! Big
white summer flats of Belsize Avenue, deep
draughts of red wine in a scheme of black clothes and pallor.
People lovely people I want to be

I feel transparent and speeded-up
I can't tell which feelings are mine
I count them like pennies: one, two, three

A sound that slurs at the edge of a plane
marks an inside and outside.
Hold up a swatch and find a match.

Yellow on red a counterpane that spins
A spiral of coloured tiles defining a crotch
I'm all around falling out and in
where two dimensions cross to three
The unstated is too patterned to be true
and hair is too fine to be seen
I'm invisible now, a maze without a mouth
The romances

the romances, their basket of light and dark,
squares teaching the moves of two games
no-one shares. The governance
of not identifying. Like catching a ball.
Like pronouncing Russian. Drained to a surface of rhythms
too vital and too clear
for any eye. That tautological
music of rage and terror and politeness.
I float above the people stating the geometry of a room,
shimmering from figure to ground, a thousand squares, a
weave, a speaker mesh pulsing and contracting
to a non-local flow, shaking out a shift of planes
I take to be nausea. I search for verticals.
Coloured by
fragments of space, watching
the snatches of myself on screen
pouring past my head fast seven and eleven,
to a rhythm I can't count.

On the way down
everything is better in black and white,
on paper or glass
a number of still frames where the music
flows in visible steps: arcane spinning
climactic.

A Long Eye

The ash keel
twirling through strata of lift
transparent to thrust
a hope the size of the wind

An eye the size of light
That missed its fall so many times;
An I the thickness of a breath
With the strike of a hawk—

The seizer of unprotected stores
As two designs fight over the surface,
A new voice unwrites the structure:
Take this life from me

Break down its mere nature
Speak the word reshaping metal,
Float the bird dispersed by the wind
Trying to grow wings as it falls.

Virtual

The arrival of software logically means
four out of five employees going but
if someone quicker grabs your market, it
goes up to five, out of five,
so you're either frantic or out of work.
There is no map of this distortion zone,
as you exist as a string not a point,
your body composed of 200 rhythms
stretches shears and fragments under heavy shocks:
you move in pieces across a broken surface.

You are what you sell and
They make you have someone sign for every hour you work
So you know
if not enough managers want you next week
You'll be out the door, *auf und davon*
So you are what you do but only an hour at a time
Borders floating
as the owners make you empty to reflect their real wishes.
If they fire more people my hourly cost goes down
and I don't get fired.

It's going to be like this for the rest of my life,
bits of me in other people's minds changing each minute
bits of me changing away from each other.

The mind moves efficiently
devolving what is solid
what is past and reliable
engaging with the necessity of good functioning
what is unfirm and undecided,
tussling over a shared model
whose nature is to be mostly unrealised states.
The real-unreal split is inoperative. How do you feel about that?

Co-ordinates of a group virtual space
mapping the solution zone
moved dexterously like a net to catch its fish
which have one more dimension than the mesh
as if it were a symbol. Language
as a transient store stuffed with
conjecture reference objects metaphors physical wishes
perceptual blocks instructions deceit
strings of other people's words
sense data dubious strings validated strings measurements
fantasies models reference patterns organized memories.
Items of different expiry, all time-based but
on a scale where wish perception action merge in one broad loop.
It is certain simply because it has lost motion.

You think your girlfriend has a delusory
world-view but there aren't tests or apparatus
for proving this and anyway your world
is falling apart day by day. She reads five books and
believes five different things at once and
subverts your awareness and judgement which have
then a one in six likelihood as she talks
and you can't disprove any of it.
How do you feel about that, Andrew?

You write poems and if a hundred people read
them you're split up into a hundred pieces
in someone else's control, on divergent courses,
and the poem is what they say, if you assert control
you're seizing authority which you can't enforce.
How do you feel about that, Andrew?

I can't sort out the way I feel from what the managers want.

Year Zero

The Invader of the Four Directions
slices through the web of causality
is transparent to the new emissions
is fear walking like a man

memorises his enemy's physiology,
cuts his kidneys out while he sleeps
climbs the stair of ruined buildings in a thousand pound suit

a spider of new webs, a surveillance grid
poured full of a new source,
a fossil pathology where star turrets
spray an angry heat, carmine cherry white washes
through a hole in the sky with an eye at its top.

Closing down
a shift of function into the older layers
new flavours pouring out of the brainstem
venoms of pure rush, heady taints
seeping into the back of the nostrils
a new signal flashes up a reptile landscape
an end zone
banded by the deserts and orchards of a new star.

Curse the Prime Minister
the ordinator of this public ritual.
May her tongue and her soul become lead,
that she may not be able to speak or act.
May she scream eternally as she screams now in rage.
As this lead is stiff and cold,
so may her heart grow cold and stop.
She's got us down for disappearing.

Curse the City and the owners of capital
I eat their eyes like fruit

I rip their guts out, wither the soft flesh along their arms;
may their parts rot while still living
may their brains fall out through their noses.
Wherever the profits go
our hands are always empty.

Curse the schools, they're so
Scared of factories, so sonorous about the wicked

I bind also the tongue and soul of
the assembler of falsehoods,
and the testimony that he brings in favour of the Right.
I consign to Demeter and Kore the man who has affirmed against me.
Whosoever makes up false simulacra of this country
and this people
let the molars of stone work on them till they are fine
let the light examine them till they are few.
I consign also
the man who has distorted my words or acts in writing
or suborned my silencing.
May he find no complaisance from the necrotic judges
when his soul shall have rotted through his flesh
but may he go before starving dogs with broken hands
and all his family with him.

Curse the bourgeoisie
cutting the machines out of the public model
in a hysteric of squeamish loathing
in a prim burst of censorship founded on interest

Curse the whole chain of knowledge
erase the mind
that had the thought

sterilise the class
that produces the culture

destroy the institutions
that gave the roles & ranks to people

burn the buildings and the symbolic texts
that set up these events
close the mouths that shape and speak them.
All these I bind, obliterate, bury, impale
and whatever claims
they may make either in the court
or before the arbitrator,
these claims shall go for nothing in deed or in word.

Year zero
a sensitive blade, tempered in cold and darkness
shape memory alloy, self-deforming to
cut out the personality
that generated the behaviour

Burn down the heritage
start again without words or buildings
there's nothing I want to preserve.

The geometry of a large scale object
with points in Sweden, Canada, New York, London
a million conscious agents
half a billion subscribers and corporate clients
is shearing into a new state
along a path of destroyed positions;
as the horizontals rip, a tiny point
somewhere on an exterior surface
travels through fracturing distortion
and my consciousness bends and snaps and sparks.
I've got two eyes seeing two different pictures
one coloured with hate, one designed by fear.
My brain's non-operational modelling
entrained paradoxes, singular matrices

Scoria sector, calcine drift
of minerals where I slip like a snake through sand
and leave nothing living; traces of life in
simmering stinking ash heaps
caches of nutrients. Bones and ruins
where vipers secrete gold and a new agent
gluts on the pathology of trapped energies
tearing protein and fat off a thigh.

You sacrificed us. Know this
When something breaks up your home
It'll have my name on it

Adjusting the Skill Mix

light seeping round corners
stood where seen and not seeing
decisive events happening at edge of
the visual sink; the dim house, the pit coped with stone.
It is over. You're wondering
What your life was, squeezing out sodden textures of
insensibility. A shaped fragment fills out
Gross errors of sense. The protractions don't match.
The notice of termination is plain.

There where the outlet pipe
drips its image, in the high office
the closing shutter oozes narrative, the crab completes its
rotary scan. cold locator, fixes measured doses
like the UV flash baking the circuit tracks onto resin.
They know where you are. Well enough.

fabulating
in darkness, lying, upset and disturbed
how can you remember what you never understood
smoothly fitting strips of lit words
focus flitting evenly in clean scans
to retell
a pleasurable story of retouched relationships
the answer is

you don't know

the sound appraising & placing you insistently
dropping its voices and receding as you hunt for it
striking your name out they
reflect in the pipe you are cleaning
as pinhole freaks bloated by mis-cues
logic fails on the impingent
smeared traces

mutilated sense in ruled space
as consciousness runs like a radio
what you sold is unsold

they pay you off

A Brush of Tow
dedicated to John Seed

a map of objects
near like a pocket or the close of your hand.
a familiar skin
fitting around the one that senses and heals
what the fingers know
the resistance, feedback
tale governing posture and grip.
a set you slip inside.

The shop as somewhere you might want to be
old custom
taking odd lengths home, immersed in it
chips from the shipyard the wrights' perk
enjoying the qualities their hands fined
a sensory and intellectual mesh
binding you into your allotted task

A list of hangings in 1740
for lifting *a silk nightgown, 7 gallons of cherry beer*
A linen apron, 2 flaxen sheets
A silver spoon a cambric mob
A ream of paper, 3 pints of rum.
you make it, it becomes another's, you take it, you die
keep your eyes down, your fingers to yourself.
The courts forcing through a new idea of ownership
a line drawn with a hempen wick.

The threshold of 1760:
The laws of property underwent
modification,
statutory expansions,
codification
in the restriction of appetite
skin and eyes sealed off

ticking to a beat of sensory deprivation
closing yourself down for the day
the empty even pulse.

As you touch it becomes what you may not touch.
Sadness and stillness paid for as a virtue
the deletion of the senses
none of us owns any of this
punished for looking, punished for wanting.
The answer to primate's curious mouth
clack jaw Margery daw picking at what is bright and soft
A long and wishing eye,
the juice dribbling around your lips.
The worker's share in the product.

Services (Polyptych)

Panel one. Sending pictures down a wire;
or, features wash away. 1978-87.

In my place graphics engines swirr
I know with my eyes shut what it's doing
paper moves back and forth, pens move left to right
spatial motors split dimensions

invested in office he paints the picture
an imaginary surface where processes are set out as lines
my senses filled   my energies replete
he is the same every day flashed, frozen, fixed
Clerk of event networks, Warden of plans
scrolls swatches of normalized space, marked
to make behaviour visible

New ideas. Counting on my fingers tells
The new on-board components will
Cut the quantity of gear by four-fifths, so
The firm's income
And then the payroll. Hungry for markets means
The rest of the world is hungry for yours.
They're quick in Sweden, they overwork in Canada.
To change, lose that shape you once had.

Thousands all around me thousands
Of bodies rushing
Through the factory gate. A torrent
dappled by cross-currents,
which threw up these buildings
Scours and sheds, slur of waste energy, breaks down
Its banks, from barriers a character came.
The river disappears. Oozy grounds loom up.
Noise and force have gone.

Panel 2: Being made redundant, November 1982; or, Intelligence.

Rooms full of objects turned to someone's design
Rooms full of words poured out of someone's heart
Millions of rooms. It's not
My hand that makes or mouth that speaks.

We've got project directors crying out for people
But it's not your name they call.
We've got workshops for the realization of dreams
But your ideas don't hold water.
A puzzle with strings and levers
food hidden for you,
in your cage.

Long monkey fingers pry apart the bark, catch the insects,
Note the repeating forms and see the causes.
The bright ones have sleek coats, wide eyes.

Mapping the parts of the complex landscape
And sensing the mental states around
In this building full of machines; you were
Emptying the world by ignorance & emptying
Your eyes and your head.
A cold monkey huddling, quiet; not curious.
You didn't catch their drift and you have to go out.

They took my job away
And what's in my head is the grip of empty hands.

They take me back because I'm a good workman.

Panel 3: updating the profile of the workforce, December, 1986; or, Overwork

They fired three out of six in my team
I wanted to protect them.
I worked till I couldn't work any more
I worked till I was lying on the floor
Of my home too tired to eat
And they fired three out of six
I can't protect anyone;
Spread out in front of the process, sheltering
Or making as if to shelter.
And covering myself. New York
Sold us off plant & livestock
And the City tore the payroll right in two.

Like a machine part thrashing in the cycle
Exploiting yourself to reach the max,
Each stroke abrades away the snibs
Till all that's left is smooth metal
Gleaming where it touches
With every surface razed.
If not for fatigue this rage would kill me
If not for rage this weariness would knock me out.
I don't even know
Am I full of hate or full of compassion
I don't even know
Why my head fills with blood.

The more they pay me
The more they take the work away from me,
I'm doing it to keep these jobs in being.
When they closed the line down in Basildon
It ripped me up.

Why're you breaking your back every day
They've got jobs stacked there blocking gangways,

Lorries standing cold in the lorry park;
They won't take your gear.

To appear in photographs. To be paid. To be a body full of motions. To have appetites and trade; to court and apply. To comply with someone's wishes, to be desired, and to be found wanting. To be bought so as to be possessed.

Panel 4: exit line.

After the years
Which filled out the physique of your obedience,
So many years that the looking back
Is like a picture to behold
As if you possessed something or could be conscious
Whatever you've got is
Because no-one would buy it off you

Whatever you belonged to
Is swilling around the streets in bits

Whatever happened to you
Your lack of awareness was part of it
And you couldn't see it where you were.

Whatever they say they want
Is what I do
Protector. Nourisher. Faithful to false commands.

Panel 5: Leaving STC, December, 1987; or, making it big.

I've seen all the numbers spooling past on a screen,
Moved with all the feelings of the workers, watching their faces.
Neither set is true
nor my words either
Nor can they agree.
I make out shapes in the data and my eye slips,
Time wipes out what was once clear.
One person can't know what the group is.
And yet I spent nine years in that big white building.
I turned my back.

There's never been trust
And we never liked each other
When we get drunk we're happy together
Eight hours a day we're like one being.
When all the relationships are ripped out
You're left with nothing but money to think on.
They fire twenty thousand people and make my career.

To the parish of Shoreditch
That's where I took my trade.
They put fine linen on my back
Set dear books in my hand;
Unstopped the airiest French wines
Put some money in my home.

Panel 6: 1986-87, mass redundancies after share price drops by ²/₃; or, Willing.

In the fog where the Alp of tinsel flared
the lies caused heat inversions in the strata of woven deceit,
the tints broke up the outline of each object,
the looped discourse garbled memory before it was stored.
The false fronts of light flashed in repeating folds,
the many-throated yammer of authority silenced
the thought of those who sought to imitate every note of that yammer.
The turning snowfall of illusory social objects
caught the loose ideas of the deceived and lost them
and we didn't notice the owners of the country failing.
They take a labour camp and turn it into a wasteland.

I wanted to make this my country, once.
Nothing happened in these buildings to remember or regret.
Routine movements, carried out fast or slow. Years of them.

When a noble family declines
The servants on the estate pursue their decay,
Courtly flounces replayed in stumbling rigmarole,
Oaf wastrels and preening vapouring sluts;
The books aren't kept and the ditches aren't dug,
The boors dance on mud floors, riot on slender means.
When you sit warm and muzzy with strong drink
It's a pleasure to think of the work undone.

They're letting go the crack-potted & the sluggards the bald-pated &
they're paying off the slacktwisted & stringy armed,
the ones who stand at a slant
they're rationalizing the dim of wit.
The great lumps are hanging round in the yard
Or coming in to get cheap meals at the canteen.
Gawping and lurching, they pass on cock-a-doodle-doo commentaries
Appraising the market niche they might address,
Puzzling at the contour of the broken planes.

They never went into the offices where the black and white
Could have told anyone they were for it.
The diagrams showing the quadrilateral where the confining lines
Of labour, cost, quality, and date allowed a fit,
The ones I plotted, transmitted, programmed, rigged,
Were never shown to them.
Yet that organized knowledge
Was nothing but their activity; their energy
Spread on axes.

The senses
filled with the location of other people's bodies
in zones of surveillance and conditioning
tracked by behavioural models
Skin tracts extended
With pattern searchers and remote sensing
Spread it out for the management.

what do you know
a shopful of folderols
and devices which while away confinement.
the number of gates girdling the capital of Shang
the starry numbers which plot the ideal city
the true story of Corineus and Belinus.

what do you know
how to assess a project & close it down
how to break down the costs and see the payroll ripped off short in
       answer
how to point to missed targets
and who was kicked out and where the jobs went

I know the City hates research and development
Short term profits, mid-term closures.
In the long run it's us or them.

What I know doesn't exist any more
I'm going to drain my senses so I can master the workings of machines

Panel 7: closure of manufacturing facility at STC New Southgate, February 1991

You shed what it was you did and
What you are dictates your life from now on but
What you did is what you are though
Now you do nothing.

They were quicker
And we clung to our rancours and privileges and
They closed us down.
Stalked & diced by a nimbler enemy.

What entrance did the failure use?
Character's the original crack
Flawlessly realized by vacant flesh;
A mis-fold in the first 16 cells of the egg
Or a bad program keyed in through the eye

The group is the circuit which empowers
Individual weakness
A rip, a craze
A slip of the knife that cut them from the red clay.
Or a fault in language making minds miss each other's path

As the object in my lens disintegrated
I reached a pitch of calm and clarity
I know every digit of what's gone wrong
I rehearse it for hours every day
I live and breathe this business.
I write off the population, who fail
Because they've been consigned to the silent roll.
Cutting out error, I'm left with a diagram.
Cord and ochre and stiff even lines.

I dream about hundreds of people, moving
With precise gestures through finely demarcated spaces

Distributed smoothly across the production surface
Calling out figures as they achieve the pattern
Seen from the cabin of a crane high above.

When I was hired there were six thousand people here.

"Then our ancient pledge will not be broken and we shall die together", said Kiso, "and now unfurl your banner, for a sign to our men who have scattered among these hills."
    —*Tales of the Heike*

The American System

Mr Evans of Wilmington, Delaware
Got his automated flour mill going in 1787
After long years of test and design.
Unhusked grain bushels at one end,
Flour barrels at the other,
No human foot set inside the building.

Already ahead in the 18th century.
A world first.
Dense thought became reality.
What gets me, they came from us,
Those superior beings. Falling away, us.

Britain using cheap labour gangs, automation no saving
Social control ahead of machine design
Let the proles do it by main force
Every institution based on cheap mass labour
Classroom discipline *shut up keep still shut up*
Every hand surrounded by warning voices
Every transgression punished and then recorded
Craftily sullen and slackly docile

I was seventeen, they gave me
A shearing machine stamped 1880
Good British gear, cut once cut true,
No power element, a counterweight and my arm's strength.
My whole life
I've seen people breaking their backs to do what
Failed because the equipment was clapped out,
The owners backing away from success.
I don't want to see this any more.
In German industry, four times as much investment per worker
New plant running clean
Over here they use musclepower and curse
Mass crews on monotonous jobs

Under surveillance with passivity
Not thinking, not cooperating
Low wage cattle from the day of their birth
Two years of rebellion 40 of compliance

Culture in lock-step with the employers
Feudalism never went away
Public praise for suppressing appetites
Applause for not crossing the lines
Motion annulled
A thousand rules penalize you for talking
The poets preach against machines
The professors teach fear of ideas
The painters paint churches and castles
Analysis jeered at, clouds of mystery furl.

It's done to hate ideas and drink all you can
Since secrecy and lies make it a poor guide
You're right to think you can't think

Year Zero, what I'm talking about

At Camden Lock

The control gate opens to destroy a state
the dark water wells and thrashes
8 foot cascades sheer fall white gush
white tracks muscling the wet saurian
eery cambers of smooth curved glass
ebb to raindrop ripples of pencil-thin
the eye searches for meaning on wan waters
as if the energy had a body.
the debris of the market resurfaces
the fairway silts up

From the first you watched your family as if from darkness
Immersed in the dense material cinema
Father, mother, restrictive lease
You pieced together numb words and speaking objects
Thousands of days left a taped regime.
Now, you wish it will never be again. Holding
A word beneath your tongue
That has no people and no things, you
Look for a place to be the outer of it.
Sighting the program to a string of numbers
You transform, shifting as their values shift
x to x' y to y'.

Among penguins and marmots, a row of monkeys
Of a dozen species, I saw each one
Fiddle with the lock or the bolt,
Imitating human fingers.
Every control gate has a fastening.
They go through what acts are possible without a forest.
I make a mental model of this special geometry.
Symbols unlatching edge of pattern cycles.

A thieves' market for chemicals clothes art and lovers.
A sluicy libido rides on complex order

Pushing everything out through the surface.
Everybody I love can be dressed here
Everything I want can be found here.
A self in the white net of the body in
The sliding planes
Shopping for missing parts.

You lie down with such travelling people who
Lose the knowledge which confines them
That was reality and your desires.
Through the erasing heads, under the darkness;
Who take you like a drug and speak a ritual
And soak in your words and looks and caress;
Who lie because memory is a shackle and
Look you in the face and do not know you.

Torpid then, sated. swelling spent. slacken and loll.
sleek black pressure head lounging towards the curl
shotglass chutes mirror rushes battered foam
under the sleeks of moss where splashes spent their course
gin yards, translucent turbine.
aligned between blue brick coamings
contact zone chokes and babbles white
flung free foamflecks dry

An Archive of 300 Poems

Every genre crumbles from within,
its heroes acquiring a character, its metres
adapted to dancing.
Every emotion comes to repeat,
a tune stirring a column of free air,
that runs
and runs into itself again
closed flow breaking at its edges

Reciting and curating 300 finished poems
Odd kilos of fragments and scrawls,
I agree with my enemies
who call off what's missing. Infinite world
shines on dull self.

a symbolic machine
that teaches you to play it
the dumb thing changing matter to hear itself
a self-entraining resonance
competing for space in the brain
by running through a film of thrilling affects
the carnal reds of rage
the autumnal blurs of sadness
a span that releases by re-starting itself:
this theatre always puts on the same play.

Diagonal scoring and pitting.
Cold shuts. Erased letters. Mirror writing.
Lead plates rolled up tightly and transfixed with nails.
Incompletion, repetition. Conjecture.
Confusion of the gods with the plane of the psychotic.
A layer of corrosion flaking away and the text with it.

The pales of the Gateway
their points clasped by bedrock

in planes of lascivious rust
boats riding, chains lapping
above the centuried strata of ooze and outfall.

Signs drowned by the landscape,
a hundred voices darting
sideways out of the mix
telltales from an It I never spoke
unspeaking my I

Searching the tape for part-patterns,
whispers to amplify.
Sonar over reefwaters.
exclusion zones describe
A solution area
free and eroded
Water I shape with a blade of flesh
in loss and confusion

Filling the white cube
with exercises of improvisation.
A broken rain of
old numbers and rigmaroles,
memorised for security, recurring
at the moment of their deletion.

Knowledge reigns on proofs of weakness
boundary lines sealed
where the energy faltered.
Strange plants:
partial metamorphoses

Edgeless recoiling flow
Genre whose heroes put on casual clothes
Imaginary space snapping its own props

Such heroes employed as puppets
Such gold-leaf winged warriors
seized by a figure-ground reversal

Shiny Circuitry

Mark worked for five years in a hi fi shop,
he merged into those shiny tiny furls of
coupled cavity loading, dither quantisation masking,
explicit lateral and depth imaging, subtle spatial clues,
horizontal glass plates flecked to break up surface standing waves,
jewel tip heated to several hundred degrees,
turntable members sizzling with suppressed whoosh,
pitless balls running in a countersunk, highly polished mirror, lost
signal buried in the null excess of the noise floor,
learnt the guitar; disappointed,
he hadn't realized that art involved feelings,
he thought clarity and sonority
CLARIT
Y
SONORIT
Y
were the end of it.
Stored with numbers
and the distinct states of equipment, couldn't
process insight and feelings: when
two signals fight over one sound stage.
Fussed by the unmeasured. Gave up the guitar.
Testing the jolt and grain (as we call it) of industrial chemicals,
he uses his whole nervous system
as a layer of self-organizing components,
circuits and output devices, to thrash at high gain.
The miracles of science in your home! such a shame
representing other people hindered
the high-brilliance solid send of libido.
Am I going to tell him
that the "human" works or can be relied on?

And art is pure. *Rhys'* painting shows
young men larking in a bathroom of some hotel,
where a plume of steam laps the flanks of silvery pipes

standing for the whole kit of urethra, spongiosa, veins, glans,
that squalid tap and bottle
he'd spent so many hours over
so many times. Soap foamed. A pleasing flow
sluiced through the conduits banded
by massive hoops. Memories, of course,
of shower stalls at school, and those temples
of rusty pipes, dark walls and basic scrawls
where brothers met over hydraulic concerns.
Deep rococo conches filled with languor,
marble facings where a pure pearl chills out and drips.
Let's not dwell on the tone values
of clean (for dirty), metal and ceramic (for flesh), stiff
(for sagging), constant flow, steam, brightness.
How much I despised that painting.

Undercapitalised

wake up in a squat with broken possessions. no-cash household
where the self swells up to be the whole week
neurology dredging up the mix of chaos and message
no good toys in this cage but the lock
eyes flick over empty pans of craving
sloughed skins of self in basal cough dust
over brick and board

we look steadily at each other exchanging
precious objects to the limit of our revenues
singing decked out in strips of shine

needle jewel, fine copper, tooled bearings
animate a volume of covert behaviour
in microgrooves a microgirl twirls
a pink froth on black gloss
people made clear and tight by fascination.
borders are everywhere their

sound shapes go away
from over wear paths,
yard-deep dust scorched by so many
toxic highs and rushes,
dissected into a pathless topology
by a cinema of
fantasy, denial

never going shopping except for
drugs, loved alms from skill's place
swallowed in tribute, king's likeness.
the bare room framing us from three sides
frond-fanned hermitage, canonical

days of absence and imitation
qualms of spit and polish

slipping along chemical gradients.
anxiety diffusing out from the pores
shudders visual surface of crustacean ooze and worms.

bored by being together
positing
substitute organs, of higher constancy and fluid pressure:
what the glass buildings despatch, other people
made bright and anxious
to make methedrine and records and IBM 3290s

Over and Over

Rhys. A vessel overflowing.
Golden and fumy; sensitive and deluded;
Opulent and musical; tragic and beautiful mind
That knows others are not true: but narrates
And narrates itself
Caring and recalling every sequin
To close out splitting views.
Once you wanted to heal the sick;
The institutions wouldn't open.
Now you tell fortunes, heal the truth,
Broken & plumed surface of the inactual
A cloth bag of black runestones. Lies about
What they most fear, the shakes and flecks of self
In dial-in reconfiguration
Language becoming a pure state.
They love this discourse adorning
Whatever impinges and refining
Ah, bright waters.

In the afternoons
You watch yourself
On TV in off-the-shoulder silk.
In a deep soft air
The pulses are slowed down to zero
Each heartbeat lasts a thousand hours
Each feeling fills the room as if with wine
In a trance where nothing is audible
The fibres soak and swell in overload
And the picture rots under the searching fluids
As beauty is born.

You hear the words of others who
Are bigots, baiters, blocked, burned out,
You left their jobs; for eight years unemployed,
In condemned homes, gay, no money; jealous.

The New Age people wheel in carts with painted scenes.
Living in miles of puzzle screens, false turns, locks for the eye.
The more often you're evicted
The more your version becomes property.
Because you're too good to be seen you stay
At home, being whoever you want to be.
Change the documents. Check
And alter the light before it gets away.

Aureate and choice and flowery and over and over
Where a thousand rays of lime converge on your face,
I switch on and goggle at the distortion,
Enhancement.
Memory is slight where
A sable-hair brush and binding symmetries
Fix and heighten every sequence
In a lavish crescendo of effects
Cut to an insistent scheme of compliance.
Is this art? is this what I do?

Where I am memory
Yielding to the designer's pencil
Using a grid composed of simple rules
My traits twist in a weird geometry
Points flick into the disappeared zone
As you drive out the unadorned me
I shiver and distort

You tell your life and it sounds like religion
You tell your lies and they feel like luxury
You preclude my voice and it feels like loyalty
You take a stand and it fades out like fading out
You have unique ideas which led you under sordor
You gaze into my soul and see someone else
You sell the truth. You studied doing me wrong.

Sitting at home crying about men, you souse; that which
Makes the organs act out operas of lies; bloated vessels
Deleting tracts of skin; so masculinity
In turned clothes
Is the hand which wounds and which heals.

Fragments of the Above

The swirl of flakes of the scene tumbling
rippling, darkening, glittering
falls out of the sky over Camden High Street
the only happiness I know or can know
a long fuselage blown across sunbeams and aimless smoke
between the Lock Market and Jamestown Road Workhouse
pieces fluttering past my hand, your mouthfuls of gnosis
whose dispersion is the stutter of your words
tip them as they fall
try to catch a life's worth

You can't find your hands
It did come out of the sky, a tile
from the roof-ridge of the Exterior.

A moment hangs in the air
between raising your foot and setting it down
the street an interior closed in a thin glass cube
the pulses so slow you can see them
of imitation taking speech and gestures like clothes
draped on the racks of the Market
of columns converging on the place to be
adornment redividing the light splashing off the body
a sexual flash like a blue wave fraying pearls of spray
in drapes of sun.
Every diagonal stands out like a track on a circuit board.
T-beam stanchions of observation platforms beside the raised way
blue pipes of scaffolding against the railway bridge
rivet-headed braces of the bridge bulkheads
windlass and key of the lock winding gear,
a moment dissolves and exhales.

Everything you want can be found here. A girl
swirling past my sight in Harlequin clothes;
the vortices of the market make your blood rush in a double-headed whirl

Filmy wings in your hand, ash
clogging in the storm-drains along Chalk Farm Road,
clings to the knots of your sweater.
You shake and eddy and blow away
a stour a swirl of separate flames
hull drawn from spiral trails
breaking up in the light it spills

Dialogue Poems

'How can an individual understand another's expressions objectively and validly? It is possible only on the condition that the other person's expression contains nothing which is not also part of the observer.'—Dilthey

The Surface of Denial

the huge coloured shapes overflow the objects
as if we were inside a surface of paint
dipped in the imaginary scene in which we
rearrange the visible fragments of process
taking the sky and repainting it blue
moving the bodies lolling in spans and masses

Deletion refines the shared object
in a squeamish selectivity
the pieces cut from the pattern freeze
as every motion is wiped out,
the surface of denial
stretches taut and opaque across a room
pale smooth refined
rips and mends at every breath
the repressed batters at the
massive wooden trap
pivoting on a slow iron staple, it
gives as we push in different directions

I hold the door closed sealing a chamber of light,
over a dissonant screen with all shapes flickering
where another life disappears in a flash of white

a shared imagined place
can be whatever we consent to,
the imperious wish
amplified to block out the room
revealing a bare and singular structure

I hold the door closed

Compliance/Intermittent Body

The stepping motor reads.
The elevated turrets swivel issuing bolts of light
Pulsed by the slats of a numbered lattice
Flashes and weals of signal
squares of image skin arriving
A sleet of painted flakes
And pulses down the nerve ducts
Compliance checked at tag intervals
Matches scanned
And the spilt signal
smeared along the aperture edges
rewritten by the perceptual filters
Fake messages transact
Not taking it in. The eye designs a corrupted model
The lines of half-shifted signal swish and blur
Two shapes fight on one surface. On
The fragile radii of the intermittent body.

Orthogonal aulic code
Six thousand years old.
Animated by metre.
Shining path of eroded marble.

The outlines of objects blend. The eye accepts
And is half of what it accepts
Waiting for the stained light to arrive.
denial of damage
Denial
Of memory sensation hope.
Aureate & exquisite & disert

Part Pattern on Grey Threads

The Before. unnamed. the movement not yet composed.
the fragments of sight and sense
before superimposition and pattern recognition
not a narrative not yet imaginary.

the slight stirs
a sheet of water divided by boards into
a net of flows
a fine sifting dust of transparent scales
stitched or severed
fade. pivot. enhance matte one. blow up.
Now the authorized account.

wood without paint: knotted grey monochrome.
Undyed canvas thread. The shuttle shoots.
desire stains and stretches and draws fine
in the distributor where sequences are stored
and issued, trying to piece
the impingent fragments of an unseen whole
sprinkling drops into the haze
part patterns on grey overlapping, coinciding

It seeps and wisps and drains
ripples
disperse along a fan of radii
the slats of the heavenly lattices slide apart
fluids pour through the spacings
the jet broadcasts during the intersect, pivots, moves on
the image wrapped over the visible
like the clothes draped over the body
like the skin forming to add nerves to the flesh
pours consolation

coarse stout threads, worn and mended

Writing on the Paper of You

I am what I write scouring and fretting
I crawl into the deep surface
I conjure ink and brushes, poured bronze characters
the membrane eats my finger spits
a new one drawn through a geometry
of strokes and gashes. a cruel fissure lattice.
the water dissolves my skin: energy hit
from canal turbidity. lost in surface shimmer.
I am what is written. star spell and meal.

the wave tracks and scans and decodes
you form a word, my lips move
I try to stand back and out
In this coarse material I begin to exist
In dull waters, cabbage leaves, faded walls
I strain to bend the lines into the shape I want

Three patterns fight over the same surface
Scrabbling at the picture plane

If We Were Immortal, If We Were Not There

Convergent lines like the struts of a crane,
Gathering parts for a tableau
That shall disperse a long carried weight

The board where inside is joined to outside
The masks rushing on a stone pitch,
The actor in a capsule of sensors and pliant cloth
whose limbs I move remotely from my couch,
whose words I utter, as
my feelings are carried on someone's hand.
Wooden eyes and phalli, stained red
Black squares bordering on silver ones
a cloud of gold smoke
swirling through a spiral slit
in 5 planes
the vexed state
    intrigued
        from simple moves
Silent rules giving birth to space
Loose company marking the great city with squares
O floodplain of wealth! O river parting all things!

A risk framed in fantasy
a swoop of slipping wings
falling and longing and flying up from fires
A night the prize of power,
heat the reward of disarming.
Success on the serried planes,
Almost in my hand the straw and living purple
almost in my belly
a violent frisson
a swollen drop of rare sensuality
a Prussian indulgence a Spartan ravishment

Who shall play the role
I do detest
Who shall devour
the feelings I do disdain

Envy and rage crown my finished game
Struggling to make a sign I can't spell
I vanish
My position without a hand or mouth

Mock heat and genuine cold.
An ideal is violated, and another has found you.
The pupa split. Rare green wing-sheaths
Flicker in a skim of new silk.
Freed from bonds of fantasy
I stand on the canal bank, in the darkness
Touched by a feeling that didn't arrive.
Empty of secrets. Out of moves.

Objects Under the Voice

full diametric scan
of the multiplanar field
coming in on 4 voices at once
this equipment is seized and shaking out a round music,
locked as a waking perimeter. the fifth voice
deflects & sweeps in as flakes of
vapourised sound. a response plane
too tiny to send its messages

a patch of bad glass shining
a patched ache
sound hidden in sound. limbless creatures
with missing voices and pure voracity
scarabs pulling their own skins off
dumb things without light which feel anger.
strangely damaged
the thwarted in three planes, thwarting

A seamless hole
before and beneath, eyeless
and skinless, nor exposed to light.
the smallest speck of chaos mouthing global lall
the melodrama waiting to strike up
the grey scenery waiting to be painted

a dim film in the mirror
a loss of light   an opacity   negative and gray
a loop caught in the beam

Acoustic Dynamics

A sonic peak. What is it? Something's being destroyed.
The loop crawls over the sound heads
I use image enhancers to bring it all out,
Blowing up the noise till I shrink to a pinpoint of awareness
Slowing it till each fleck is a long black smear.

Three tracks fight over a volume:
The genuine signs, which had sources
My hypotheses, which dressed the powdery data
The motor noise of my head grinding what it takes in.

Those precious few inches of tape in their
Mirror image shell halves, perfect circles,
Are all I can know of you, but cannot be read.

In my acoustically null chamber,
I fill in the squares of memory.
My black glass cupola slows and snares
Every grain of light with its blankness and wetness.
I lose the surface and see the material prehuman.
As if I had let something escape, I let nothing escape
I slow down the playback till it is almost frozen,
Head down snuffling for every speck of dust,
Stripping my skin to make it more sensitive,
Rerunning the visual-hormonal chains,
Looking out for feedback gains
As if the unused meanings contained subversion and wealth,
As if a second order could catch fire from part-patterns,
But every simulation had the same outcome.

The bearers of rain come close to their falling,
The vessels are near to losing what they know.
When the levee breaks,
The wet masses of earth surge and run.
The orchards swell beneath the pents of flood.

All I want is your compliance, all I want
Is for you to be someone else.
We pick up the river in a net. It's gushing it's falling it's gleaming and
    bucking.

I take the sound chains and fit them into
A theoretical shell. What is she like?
Because her life is empty
She fell in love
Because this city hasn't occupied her
Because she has no hopes
She tells fortunes all day.

Your signs relate to acts we never carry out,
My personality which you have invented as you wished,
Magical acts, systems of divination,
Or something else for which no control exists.

Tatterdemalion red and yellow, floating
Cloak of patches where the eye loses its way
The water meadow is sometimes flood,
A sheet of ripples and reflections, sometimes
Mud, a haze of fever and chills, sometimes
A summer island, raft of flowers. The water
Washes away bounds or edges or memory.

In traces
I find the half-made impulses.
Putting the Fourier space on a screen and snapshotting it
I find persistent outlines suggesting objects.
Yet there's nothing here I want,
No quality I could linger on.
I hate every single idea in your head,
I couldn't jump in the water
I jumped in the water, it wouldn't touch me.

When I was a child I had a gunsight:
A still frame against which deviation can be tracked.
Prussian glass, looted from their King; of equable temper;
With a spirit level, to locate the vertical,
To define the powder of light infalling;
A compass, tense iron, to locate the North;
A grating, to measure not just angles, but also,
Its notched scale, convert magnitude into absolute distance,
And translate the small cipher of the glass eyeful
Onto the large cipher of the observer's map;
Sight wires, to straighten wavering wrists;
The chanciness and fleetingness of events
Were caught as if with swords. Error steadied.
The ordnance flew straight and true.
I watched the hills above the town
I was close I was far away.

I could see but not be touched.
The charges flicker on the pleasure heads.
The weary toils of starlight slide down the worn paths,
The cups fill and free the tall cataracts.
The buildings are weeping,
Openings piercing their tight orthogonals,
The shoals of water slip through the meshes.
Their baked clay roils about to spill.
The heavenly electricity flashes on the wash.

The event is here
What the screens are breaking down really is love.
Attenuated shut space of display screen.
Where energies distort or are deflected
I am in this picture, I hear the clips like
A truth too cruel to be spoken, lies that will not
Be quiet: you always talked, five people
In one head. Why did you never know,
With your witch books, your bag of bird bones,
What my intuition was?

Why weren't you afraid of me?
Because I repressed every sign.

Because I have no hopes
I wind back the tape and restart it.
After 20 generations of filtering
All I can hear is the pinwheel motor noise,
An even grey flood
Wrapping and drugging me.

Hallucination and Mutilation

Part 1: Psilocybin

You wanted to run the river through your hand
and take the poison out of it.
You saw broken stones
and wanted to make them whole again.
You took your reason which held you back
and wiped it out.

You took the mycoid hallucinogen
Every day for ten weeks, gouging
A hole in your mind to let feelings in:
Till you had the Pythian intuition
To see the future and the heart; that hole
Never heals and cannot seal. You called
The invisible by its right name. Human chemicals replaced
So that a splinter of wood makes you see forests,
A drop of rain makes you see fountains for half an hour;
The tiniest
Whispers breathed out a landscape; you drank the meanings
From the crass unsteady stream
Like gulps of wine. Then, the fungus
Gave you asthma and the fever dreams
flew breath over breath,
Flashing and rippling hypervivid scream
Until your lung collapsed. Thin, withered,
Lungless, mad, with sight of souls,
You fled from reason to a moor of wraiths.
They tracked and ate you.

In the economic frame
Subjectivity is a disease. Which kills our insides
But since that frame is firm, your subjectivity
Is like an illness and the first phase of getting killed.

Star rise star fall: hissing in a pool
When all nations shall change to a pure language
In which the meaning of love is clear, transforming
Their lips their skins their hearts and way of moving
And our flesh falls away; the star incidence
Foretold by the scrier casting twigs upon a cloth.
Woman, don't throw a lot on me.
Anyone who hears those words
Should know the truth they'll never hear again

Anyone who cuts a tender fabric
Must drink whatever waters flow

Anyone who lingers at the boundary finds
To go to the spirits is to lie
Down among the dogs and flies.

I am your ideal as
The food of spirits is the leavings of flesh.
What I know, I learnt it from you
Each day we spent together
I became more like you, being soaked up
Till I built a wall across:
Here is the line of division, carved
With the slashes of a harsh decree:
Here I end, and here the world ends.
I tore you apart. I can't feel any pain.

Love is a pearl beyond price but that's
What you have instead of me. When I'm cut,
You bleed.

Call not that which ye cannot send back.
Wound in words that made
Your eyes bright, you didn't ask
Who leaves such lures and lark-mirrors
Or what food they live off.

Spiritual and sexual greed
Are organic strength
Or thorough deficit, I can't fix
Which. It's like watching
A river swallow rain and leaves and outfall pipes.
I most want to be a good engineer.

You taught me about myself,
Your perception is finer than all others, I mean
You let more in and the part patterns
Which measurement is too slow for and
Lucidity too bright to accept;
As muscle impulses before they are flickers or
Ideas when they are insects flitting across a floor and
Emotions far beneath a frozen surface.
A torn membrane right across the room
Flapped by a sucking breath.

Part 2

I. The Crystalline Structure of North London

An eye outside the pit of gravity
Fixes this whole island with steady gaze,
From a steelmaking city where the big furnaces
Like stars melt and enrich metals in a gloss of flame
To a Western archipelago where the backs of islands
Surface like vast lizards basking in the ocean,
As the gulls slice through the drapes of Hyperborean light:
The loved object is held still and clear.
Out there where the unbelievable sparseness
Stabilizes an eye with no pulse or muscle shake,
Components insulated by ceramics, connected by gold,
Set to a tolerance of thousandths of an inch
Change state with each flake of impingent light!

Where the waste heat of the flesh is error
The meticulous germanium detectors are true and steadfast.

Riegl said, the struggle for existence
Darkens the harmony of forms, disturbing
With its squeezing of nerves, its projections,
The crystalline symmetry of art and nature.
Geometrical form is the adequate condition of art.
So animal and human natures
Warp the underlying crystal lattice,
Rich in symmetries, feather furled by force.
I glimpsed a crystalline structure
Investing the whole of North London:
Without projection or blocks, without passion or trauma,
No distension or aversion or fantasy or colouring,
Without wish;
A true mapping that gives and holds.

Nine years ago I came to this city in three lacks.
Up on the range where
Left politics, obscure poems, unrequited love
Lifted me in one serial high.
I saw a perfect society
Where structure becomes story
As free motion is even and unbroken. Sensory
Deprivation is the key, opening
Antiworlds in whose yards the mind is trained.
I said and thought a million words
As if the words had hearers or the ideas brick and stone.
The daedal coneries of language led me a fine dance.
Starved by the true, wasted by the Lie
I built a system with three parts
Of world, rage, and depression, not knowing
What existed around me; with broken glass for eyes.

Calvin warns us in the *Institutes*,
The Holy Ghost has a way into the heart,

Without passing through the air,
To expound the knowledge of the path.
Other demons there are, excrement of the world spirit
Conductors on paths and commanders of sweet voices,
Whose nature suits the weaknesses of men,
Passing through the flesh like wine.
Their skill is imitation and deceit.
Emptiness and longing are satiated
With illusions more patterned and detailed than outer sense,
Flooding in edgeless profusion.
And as you walk in the strips of puzzling light
No desire is fulfilled
No action completes its course.

A fortune cast. An echo off the faces saying
Andrew. conformist and technophile, meticulous and numb,
idealistic and overstressed, remote and Puritan,
secretive and formalistic. solitary and fearful.
cold and exact and furious about error.
Nine years in the same engineering firm
breaking up now through technical errors;
A pattern within a mind disintegrates
complete

Oh, empty hands and empty head.
Dispelled by Time the signified of Hope emaciates
A message; cool white track
Of life energy
Out in silence and darkness towards the stars.
I engraved a singular matrix, an unrealizable geometry.
All my emotions died then. Externalized mapped and buried.

II.

What I have in mind first is unrequited love,
A distortion of the inner organs.

Chained in this disputed object,
We struggled for its control.
Reality burst out of that conflict,
A strange trajectory as two patterns
Consume and recode each other.

Starvation fired me up. Then took my appetite from me,
Habit acts to change the melancholic lover
Into someone cold and pedantic
As excess ripens into excess. My heart is empty.
Every summer the apples by my window fall
On the concrete court where the drying-lines are,
Every year I am sad watching them and myself rot
As ruined genetic material.
A hole on the surface of the eye
Darkens the harmony of natural forms.

I remember before there were events
I lived in a house full of people and animals
As one of a family, it was never quiet.
I couldn't tell myself apart from what happened.
But now I live alone
Both the air and my soul are silent.
I drench myself in art and work and drink,
The sombre observances of hierarchy and fantasy.

III. Poetry and Fame

Freeing language, I
Erected an asymmetry with no truth nor listener.
I recited from the book called *Red Skin*.
With a thin knife I opened the edge of my body.
The bowl shakes with no mover. Lips open in its silver.
"Called by name, thrilled by your bell,
I attend, and drink the terrestrial juice
Whose nutrients I need to keep my wings aloft.
What is my night's work, Magister?"

A. Bring me a Russian forest: black, resinous, piny, birchy,
A fleet of masts, dreaming, ninety days across, with
Faint sounds of aurochs, marten, sable, and bear;
With honeycombs and pools where it sees itself; where
Trees are buried and seeds fly on their single wing;
Where nine cats sing in nine languages;
Where the naked witches eat agaric pulled from under-boles.

Demon. "Name each part and I will build it in this night.
You must know how I lost my heavenly place
For the fine movements of flesh
So enticed me that I learnt how to eat.
Weak with satiation
I obey and deceive. Fallen
And of mixed nature, I regret
The light I can no longer see."

A. Bring me a storm of whirling petals!
Bring me a ship of pure white on a sea of ice!
Bring me the song, falling from a bird's rare beak,
Bring me the very device within which we are confined!
Bring me a Greek city, laid out on a straight Hippodamian grid,
Its perspectives rolling into a vertical drama,
Dropping in vast tiers from the mountaintop to the harbour mole!
In the forum the aretalogi are spinning their tongue-
Twisters, lubber-dazzlers, glass-glint, Gorgian figures.
Out of the water like reflections out of their
Mirror, on trestles splay a haul of skewed body plans:
Eels, squid, cuttlefish, mussels, sea-urchins.
As new bronze castings are knocked—dull, hot—out of the birth sand,
The master mason chisels the temple design onto a single block,
The cypher-maze which the whole site team follows.
The men are fixing ribs to an upside-down boat,
Like carpenters nailing battens to a roof-tree.
The shepherds' beehive huts… but what! these walls
Are crumpling, their tints are growing dim.

Demon. "My limbs are weary, I cannot sustain
Your commands. I strike my sets of glass,
These tattered papers the only trace.
Your fit leaves you white and shaking, eyes red.
As the dawn fills your window with faint light
I too must leave these measures with regret
Before a day of weeping."

IV. A Perfect Society

I appreciate
What Burke said about an organic, nonrational society,
In this sense, that our *nature* is violence and deceit.
Animal desires wreck the parity of pristine forms.
Revolution arises from hallucination,
The *champ d'élection* of the deceiver.
Weakness is not made public in physical contest
But in lie and counter-lie, through scores of inversions,
Ideas competing for sites in dissonant maps,
Agents playing false cards in their puzzle canon.
As reasoning and languaged beings
We reached our actual price by disputing in this way.
Where every rule *assumes* the wish to deceive
The financial markets toss and sort out
The clever from the simple: by hearing.
Spending and engaging in a vast artificial landscape
Led by human mouth, you reached your station.

Then when deception and memory fail
And estate walls are torn up and status un-named
The first instants
Supply already the persuader with his designs,
Building the false knowledge which is power;
By day three you are both possessed and driven.
What most we long to possess
Is other people. What most threatens us
Is other people's power. We become wealth, complying.

Those states brought us our state and bring it
To exchange for itself.
I no longer wish a better policy,
I just want everyone to have food and
A roof over their heads when it's cold:
A country I never lived in, a design
Which excels the grasp of my imagination
And has no ground in my senses.
Such a longing draws my tendons out long and thin.

V. A Doketic Cosmos

The power to choose chooses what reason reaches.
I took in the world through my senses
in momentary flashes, from cramped lines of sight,
changed at once into stores
sharing the characteristics of the storage medium,
edges lost in seep or surge.
Frozen protein turns to glass, as constant;
unlevel man, with long head and short skull,
does history change every time you have a mood?

You must know what the Persians taught,
that the universe is for the five elements a clinic
where they may be cured, for the breed of demons
a prison where they may be kept under restraint.
The cosmos we are born and live in is factitious,
the material labour of the Demiurge who walks
in deceit and violence, snared in the fogs and dusks,
the green we see is not the real green
the light we are informed by is not the real light
the place we live in is not our real home
our eyes have such a weakness locking us
in His superfluity of askance mimic forms,
puzzles lures snares.
Just so the physical affect of Depression

seals off the senses to reduce the doses of pain.
O unceasing sun, whose bolts jump straight,
each new gasp of your light is the truth
trapped
as the turbid affects of the body ferment
blur a miserable hallucinatory cosmos

Paper traces of the illness remain, visible
passages of a perverse geometry; glimpses
of monstrous organs, rending jaws of demons,
hooks on their nipples; green pitted skin
of false conceptions shaped by lust, scenes
in the film of hatred; decades of servitude;
swarms of vermin animating a dulled brain.
One stores memory
in cells which change state. Society
is too large to be seen, and I am too unsteady.

VI. Renouncing Demons

Skin too cold to feel pain, the warrior
Is reborn at the end of ages.
Pent in my circle, skimming a crystalline surface of metal
To perfect the geometry of an external Sign,
I think of the women who used to love me.
How fine to be the weakness of the weak, to be
That thing the suffering imagine in their sufferings.

In this shine I see rows of audience,
Each one like Ruth, in my diagram, to hear
These traces I make and lose their hearts to me
As I pace out the measures of my arrogance.
Admiration is a folly. Why should I
Hammer smooth the leaf that sheathes an illusion
Or paint the soaring pinions of my vanity?
Gazing into your weakness the stronger Other

Bends you to His idea,
Incising the image and denaturing you.
You are deceived. Art is a fever, a distension.
A denial
Blows out the membrane where images form
Reflecting nothing, drafted by want
As vapour by cold air.
I have seen monsters race across my eye,
I have been tormented,
Strained in fetters five;
I have seen the devil in a wood, I have seen
The very instrument of our deception.

Identity is desire
Desire is a lack.
In this still mirror I catch my own image:
Lost and starved,
Poised and perfect
Tranquil in shock and chill.
I'd have it so. This is not anyone else.

VII. Tuyau as Heat Lens

blind cones focussing crushed light
falling in. ray becoming solid object.
a convergence of straight lines
beating the universe into a pattern
by a distortion of the inner organs
seizing an emotional property, tapering
trapping past and future in a hot solid.
mesmeric certainty. asthma. fever.
furnace throat blocking up.
breathe in the ash pit, blow
those supple flakes. strophes of
prophetic rage. cells turgid, swashing heat.
cult division and private code

an interpretative school. an autonomy.
rigid with message, clenched with destiny
uttering irrevocable gold charges
a hysterical cone burning what it swallows

a ripple of chill
as your inside disappears
and a remote stable world stretches itself out
in four directions
signless shapeless selfless
ochre field
      like the ash
           of a lost paranoia

The lens with a thousand parts
is disassembled waste light
wringing out of it in rolls
The bursting of the cell wall
the loss of precious inner narratives
of knowledge and an idea of character
The loss of cinnabar, pine resin, and medlar pulp
the inner waterways
so numerous in their openings
so rich in dissolved substances

A room of glass cases
A face that slips away
storing relics of wholes that never existed
a slab of inlet fossils
clean sliced and polished high
A sequence of words
scored in an image complex
tapering to the furnace shoulder

VIII. Re-cut, Re-score

Measure a pound of cloud
or, find the last in the set of curves.
Riegl writes the whole history of ornament,
Haton de la Goupillière worked,
in Coimbra, Portugal,
on the set called nautiloid surfaces.
Let the sea surge do his research.
Code them all in a roll of numbers—
a tear-off sheet, could we ever run out?
this one the turn of a chambered shell
this one, the line of a certain actress's shoulder and neck
this one, the catenary of a bridge at Clifton
this one, the recessed and split globes of a mosque roof
this one, the teasing disorder of a certain Kashmiri textile—
but all curves exist before they are drawn
in a universe we broach that transfigures us
and spits us out.

perspective as loss
edged eyes betraying radiant light
Draw out a lens at its edges
to form a sphere
with a spherical tube
areal light
flowing into film as liquid or as record
drowning surfaces, capturing, released

a geometry where I am cut in segments
going from the office to the shop and the pub,
filling a place in a sequence,
emitting myself as a message
drowned in the sound that others give off

sites states
scores of a circular collaborative music.

the vantage of one who looks down
as if from the roof garden of a High Street pub
on the throng, through no-one's pair of eyes,
catching the shape running across the crowd,
a motif repeated from a physics textbook?,
a figure of birds catching the wind;
as if seeing eddies on great waters
drift and scour, giving off sound
human networks may grow in curves,
a personal knowledge might grow in a spiral.
any partial moment
takes away a broken cycloid,
no-one's marble detail.

The cutting and matching shop
where the rises and falls of the aged
cadences that are what we know of time,
its complete language with five words
gold, mercury, apples, cloth, silk,
its cycloid shapes that return to the first,
and what the outer senses tell of falling words,
of light shining off faces, of
buildings and peopled streets,
are married together, and by a
heretic unstitched:
mouth closes on mouth circling
around straight language.

dark tangles of cement and cable
where separate spaces join.
a list of movements for the camera motor
written down before the action
the emergence of a personality
in the distribution of cuts and joins
repetitively running through
the scenes mandated by the genre rules—
the shooting of one plane of colour into another,

the depiction of the male Eros
in curves of the trouser *bouffant*.

Cubes of virtual space
projected from a darkened script.
Tectonic holes
permitting a new country.

Personality Inventory 10.1.88

the idea of freedom
the idea of an identity outside other people
the idea of not having to work all day
the idea of imperatives coming from within

A year working on
An export project, for the US.
The UK market is too small to pay for research,
It's export or disappear. I wanted that project
As nothing else

The Canadians bought 25% of our firm, made a deal,
They fold my project.
My boss resigned. I bow to superior force.
They signed a contract saying we aren't allowed to compete.

The idea of a colony. Servants have
no honour, nor is there
any order here
save fixing of the owners' wishes,
as deep camouflage to avert violence.
I think about what is not true.

Folk life without capital or research
a wild strip between two bare fields.
four weeks, between jobs.
your eyes to cry with.

I'm winding up
to hurt someone and not be hurt. Numb
the blade before cutting.

I thought about this the first day I met her.
Gave feelings time to flower,
now it's time to cut the wires. Wipe

her off my lens. I couldn't react as I wanted.
I make her unemployed.

Their big emotions scare me
and crowd me out. Without policy
I follow and do not believe.
I can't hear my feelings in the noise.
For me private life is like work.

Somebody somebody owns or somebody
who owns
nothing

Flesh pulse
like something so hurt and shocked
it hides and can't be lured.
Whatever I look at
I can't see.

What I had
I sold it. Drained glass.

I left my job.
When the lights go away
when the people go away

The idea of thermodynamics
in this flat for example
the water heater's broken.
Blue and shivering if
I lack money so do what they want then.
If I were as cold as the air around
I would not lose small domestic gusts of heat.
Small domestic lumps of capital.

Marshalling yard. Road out, order made up
cif Wilson Street, EC2. Check the papers: what

but the bits of people I used to know,
unspent halves of the double moving being?
Space bursts from around the body, patterns
pressed by many humans moving and emitting.
Now they're gone. Will anything happen inside me?
or is it just inside them?
Withdrawing.
Shaky contact, smears and wisps
receding surface of symmetry broken
curved matching plate slipping away.
singular facets. Image unshapes.

There's nowhere I can go
to feel or possess or enjoy.
Chilling the skin.

The room walled with fantasy
A white powder, a bag of money.
Hitting the Americans and stealing their trade.
A painting
a special painting of fine and binding lines
opulent and neurotic
a painting by a young man
of flowers and women and sweet water
swirls of sheer colour slighting the bounds of objects
patches of white space pure and not filled.
An idea
a hot bath
the room where everything is true

My face in the mirror
wrapped in sweetness and pallor
around a block of bloody rancour.
Effeminate. Distant. Blank.

1992/1995

www.ingramcontent.com/pod-product-compliance
Lightning Source LLC
Chambersburg PA
CBHW031154160426
43193CB00008B/357